THE
YOGA-SUTRA
OF
PATANJALI

THE
YOGA-SUTRA
OF
PATANJALI

TRANSLATOR

MANILAL NABHUBHAI DVIVEDI

GYAN

Published by

GYAN

Gyan Publishing House
5, Ansari Road
Daryaganj, New Delhi-110002
Phone: 011-47034999, 9811692060
E-mail: books@gyanbooks.com

Distribution Network
gyanbooks.com
India, USA, Canada, UK, Australia

ISBN: 978-93-6920-039-9 (PB)

First Published, 1890

2nd Impression 2025

Printed at: Gyan Press, Delhi.

THE YOGA-SUTRA OF PATANJALI
Translator: MANILAL NABHUBHAI DVIVEDI

THE

YOGA-SUTRA

OF

PATANJALI.

(Translation, with Introduction, Appendix, and Notes based upon several authentic commentaries.)

BY

MANILAL NABHUBHAI DVIVEDI,

Sometime Professor of Sanskṛta, Sâmaladâsa College.

PUBLISHED BY

TOOKÁRÁM TÁTYÁ

FOR THE BOMBAY THEOSOPHICAL PUBLICATION FUND.

PREFACE.

THE following pages are prepared with the view of replacing Govindadeva S'âstri's translation of the *Yoga-Sutra* published by the Theosophical Society. Owing to the too literal method followed by the translator that book is of little use to the general student. The American revision of it is no improvement, inasmuch as it is not based on accurate study of the original. Dr. Rajendralâl Mitra's scholarly translation pubished in the Calcutta Asiatic Society's Series is a literal rendering of Bhoja; and is open, more or less, to the objection of not being useful to the general reader. With the view, therefore, of preparing a clear explanation of the *Yoga-Sutras* suited to the wants of the general reader, without omitting whatever is critical in the several commentaries, I have prepared the following. I have given a literal translation of the Sutras adding explanatory notes drawn from various sources. I have taken care to avoid the subtle discussions in which Vijnânabhikśu's *Yoga-Vârtika* abounds, but at the same time I have tried my best to put in as simple a form as I can, the results of some of the important issues raised by that accurate scholar. My notes are based on the *Bhâśya* ascribed to Vyâsa, the commentaries of Vâchaspatimiśra, Bhoja, and Râmânanda-Saraswati, and the *Yoga-Vârtika* of Vijnânabhikśu. I have derived no mean help from Dr. Rajendralâla's and Govindadeva S'âstri's translations, as also from the Marâthi translation of Râmânanda-Saraswati's *Maṇiprabhâ* by the learned S'âstri Râjârâma Bodas of Elphinstone College, Bombay. My best thanks are due to these scholars. There are a few points where I have thought it necessary to differ from one or other of these; and the careful reader will be able to note and judge the improvement as he reads. The *Yoga* is more a practical than a theoretical science. I cannot pretend to decide upon the merit of any particular rendering on the strength of practical experience. I have, however, compared all the versions available and have decided in favour of one or the other. My best guides in this matter have been Vyâsa, Râmânanda-Saraswati and Vijnânabhikśu.

There are two opinions as to the authorship of the *Sutras*. In fact PATANJALI is not the author, but the compiler of the philosophy in the set of *Sutras* before us. Several scholars are of opinion that this Patanjali is not the same as the author of the *Vyâkaraṇa-Mahâbhâśya* ; while others take the contrary opinion. The date and a few facts of the life of Patanjali, the *Bhâśyakâra*, are pretty certainly known ; as to the other Patanjali, if there be one, we are yet in the dark. I have nothing new to add to what has already been achieved by eminent scholars in this direction ; and I would refer curious students to their writings on this head.

NADIAD,
9th June 1890.

M. N. DVIVEDI.

ERRATA.

PAGE.	LINE.	INCORRECT.	CORRECT.
7	8	possession	passion
„	20	perfect devotion	with perfect devotion
11	28	XVIII.	XIX.
13	19	descrimination	discrimination
25	8 & 10	refers	refer
37	24	active on that his,	active through him,
43	24	has the entire	has for its end the entire
53	15	consist of the phenomenon	consists of the phenomenal
56	23	its	it
58	27	drop	droop
59	21	become	becomes
65	13	disserves	dissevers
66	9	consist	consists
69	8	*Samayama*	*Samyama*
74	10	word	words
77	16	*Bhutendviyajayi*	*Bhutendriyajayi*
85	17	dertroy	destroy
88	30	independantly	independent
93	3	it, the	it is the

INTRODUCTION.

A SYSTEM of ethics not based on rational demonstration of the universe is of no practical value. It is only a system of the ethics of individual opinions and individual convenience. It has no solidity and therefore no strength. The aim of human existence is happiness, progress, and all ethics teach men how to attain the one and achieve the other. The question, however, remains what is happiness, and what is progress? These are issues not yet solved in any satisfactory manner by the known systems of ethics. The reason is not far to seek. The modern tendency is to separate ethics from physics or rational demonstration of the universe, and thus make it a science resting on nothing but the irregular whims and caprices of individuals and nations.

In India ethics has ever been associated with religion. Religion has ever been an attempt to solve the mystery of nature, to understand the phenomena of nature, and to realise the place of man in nature. Every religion has its philosophical as well as ethical aspect, and the latter without the former has, here at least, no meaning. If every religion has its physical and ethical side, it has its psychological side as well. There is no possibility of establishing a relation between physics and ethics but through psychology. Psychology enlarges the conclusions of physics and confirms the ideal of morality.

If man wants at all to understand his place in nature, and to be happy and progressing, he must aim at that physical, psychological and moral development which can enable him to pry into the depths of nature. He must observe, think, and act; he must live, love, and progress. His development must be simultaneous on all the three planes. The law of correspondence rules supreme in nature; and the physical corresponds as much to the mental, as both in their turn correspond to the moral. Unless man arrives at this stage of corresponding and simultaneous development on all the three planes, he is not able to understand the meaning and importance of his existence, or existence in general; nor even to grasp the idea of happiness or progress. To that man of high aim whose body, mind and soul act in correspondence, the higher, nay even all, secrets of nature become revealed. He feels within himself, as everywhere, that universal Life wherein there is no distinction, no sense of separateness, but, therefore, all bliss, unity, and peace.

This peace is the peace of spiritual bliss (*Mokśa*). The course of nature never ceases, action always compels even the peaceful *to act*; but the individual being already lost in the Individual, the All, there is nothing unpleasant to disturb. The peace of spiritual development is indescribable, and so are its powers indescribably vast. As you go on forgetting yourself, just in the same proportion do spiritual peace and spiritual powers flow in towards you. Take the ordinary illustration of sleep or hypnotism or mesmerism. Dreams, often real dreams, clairvoyance, and a number of similar phenomena are possible simply because the organism is free from individuality and is, for the time, attuned to the strings of the Individual. But these states lead, on account of the absence of positive spirituality, to the evils of irresponsible mediumship. The rule, however, is clear that extinction of individuality is the only way to real progress and peace. When one consciously suppresses individuality by proper physical, mental, moral, and spiritual development, he becomes part and parcel of the immutable course of nature, and never suffers.

All philosophy has this four-fold development and spiritual peace in view. In India there have been six such schools of thought. Each starts with a more or less rational demonstration of the universe, and ends with a sublime code of ethics. There are first the atomic (*Vaiśeśika*) and the dialectic (*Nyāya*) schools, seeking mental peace in devotion to the ruler of the universe. Then there are the materialistic (*Sânkhya*) and the practical (*Yoga*) schools, teaching mental peace by proper analysis and practical training. Lastly, there are the orthodox (*Mimânsâ*) and the unitarian (*Advaita*) schools, placing spiritual bliss in strict observance of Vedic injunctions and in realising the unity of the Cosmos.* It will thus be seen that the *Yoga* is a complement of the *Sânkhya*, and that therefore a clear idea of the latter is indispensable to a proper understanding of the former.

The *Sânkhya* is an enumeration (*sânkhyâ*) or analysis of the universe. It starts with the proposition that the world is full of miseries of three kinds, physical (*âdhibhautika*), supernatural (*âdhidaivika*), and corporeal (*âdhyâtmika*); and that these are the results of the properties of matter (*prakṛti*) and not of its inseparable correlate intelligence of consciousness (*puruśa*). The inseparable *prakṛti* and *puruśa* are enough in themselves to account for the whole of the phenomena of the universe, and the idea of a Creator is looked upon by the Sânkhyas as a mere redundant phantom of philosophy. *Puruśas* are each a centre of simple consciousness, being ever unchangeable and unique. *Prakṛti* is that substratum wherein the three properties, passivity(*sattva*), energy or activity(*rajas*), and grossness (*tamas*), exist in a state of equilibrium. Energy moves the other two and evolution begins. From the first differentiation of *prakṛti* proceeds *mahat* or the germ of individuality which gives birth to *Ahankâra* or individuality proper. *Ahankâra* from its passive and gross sides produces, under the influence of energy, the eleven organs of action and perception, internal and external,† and the five states (*tanmâtras*)‡ preceding material formation. From the *tanmâtras* are evolved the five definite material

* For particulars about these six, see introduction (Sec. II.) of my *Râjayoga* (second edition), and my "Monism or Advaitism?" (Sec. II.)

† The five *jnânendriyas* + the five *Karmendriyas* + the *manas*.

‡ *Rupa, rasa, gandha, sparśa, śabda.*

elements, *âkâśa*, *vâyu*, *tejas*, *jala*, *pṛthvi*, the five states of matter properly speaking, which enter into the formation of *things*. These are the twenty-four *forms* of *prakṛti* which, with the *puruśa*, make up the twenty-five elements into which the *sânkhya* resolves the whole of the universe.

All pain is the result of *rajas*; all grossness, ignorance, darkness, of *tamas*; all pleasure, passivity, knowledge, peace, of *sattva*. The mind is a result of *rajas*, and it is *sattva* alone which by its light illumines it and enables it, at times, to catch glimpses of the blissful *puruśa* ever near to *sattva*. This point will be amply cleared in the *yoga-sutras*; and the distinction between, and the necessity of, mind, *sattva*, and *puruśa*, will also be explained (sec. IV.). The point here is to show what is meant by the spiritual peace aimed at by the *Sânkhya*. All experience consists of mental representation, the *sattva* being clouded, obscured, or entirely covered over, by the nature or property of the representation. This is the root of evil. The act of the mind cognising objects, or technically speaking, taking the shape of objects presented to it, is called *vṛtti* or transformation. It is the *vṛtti* which, being coloured by the presentation, imparts the same colour by re-presentation to *sattva*, and causes evil, misery, ignorance, and the like. All objects are made of the three *guṇas*; and when the *vṛtti* sees everywhere nothing but *sattva*, to the exclusion of the other two, presentation and representation become purely *sâttvika*, and the internal *sattva* of the cogniser realises itself everywhere and in every thing. In the clear mirror of *sattva* is reflected the bright and blissful image of the ever-present *puruśa* who is beyond change, and supreme bliss follows. This state is called *sattvâpatti* or *mokśa* or *kaivalya*. For every *puruśa* who has thus realised himself, *prakṛti* has ceased to exist; in other words, has ceased to cause disturbance and misery. The course of nature never ceases, but one who receives *knowledge* remains happy throughout, by understanding the Truth. The *Sânkhya* tries to arrive at this result by a strict mode of life accompanied with analysis and contemplation.

This state of peace, besides being conducive to eternal calm and happiness, is most favourable to the apprehension of the truths of nature. That intuitive knowledge which is called *Târaka*, a word mistranslated or rather misunderstood as a particular star by Dr. Rajendralâla and others, puts the student in possession of almost every kind of knowledge he applies himself to. It is indeed this fact on which the so-called powers of *yoga* are based.

The *yoga* subscribes to the *Sânkhya* theory in *toto*. The *yoga*, however, appears to hold that *puruṣa* by himself cannot easily acquire that *sâttvika* development which leads to knowledge and bliss. A particular kind of *Iśvara* or supreme God is therefore added for purposes of contemplation, etc., to the twenty-five categories of the *sânkhya*. This circumstance has obtained for *yoga* the name of *Seśvarasânkhya*, as *Sânkhya* proper is called *Niriśvarasânkhya*. The second and really important improvement on the *Sânkhya* consists in the highly practical character of the rules laid down for acquiring eternal bliss and knowledge. The end proposed by *yoga* is *samâdhi* leading to *kaivalya*. *Yoga* and *Samâdhi* are convertible terms, for both mean *vṛttinirodha* or suspension of the transformations of the thinking principle. *Samâdhi* is of two kinds, *savikalpa* and *nirvikalpa*, called *samprajnâta* and *asamprajnâta* in the text. The first, generally speaking, is that wherein the mind is at rest only for the time, the second is that wherein, through supreme universal non-attachment, it is centred in *Sattva*, and realises *Sattva* everywhere, for all time. The mind being, as it were, annihilated, *puruṣa alone* shines in native bliss. This is *Kaivalya*. *Prakṛti* has played itself out for that individual *puruṣa*.

This is the end in view. This, in fact, is the meaning of happiness and progress, the end and aim of all science and philosophy. This conclusion is deduced as a direct corollary from the theory of evolution set forth at the beginning. The intermediate stages relate to the ethics prescribed in conformity with these. The stages for reaching this state are eight in number. *Yama*, *niyama*, *âsana*, *prâṇâyâma*, *pratyâhâra*, *dhâraṇâ*, *dhyâna* and *samâdhi*. These are fully described in the text and the appendix. The first two are rules aiming at simultaneous physical, intellectual, and moral elevation, leading to spiritual peace. The next two or three are practices preparing the mind for steady concentration on, and continued application to, any thought or object. The last three are continuations, varying in degree, of the same process, and ending with *samâdhi*, i. e., *nirvikalpa-samâdhi*, which is *kaivalya*.

It may be argued all this is exclusive mental or moral development; but it should not be forgotten how intimately the mind and the body are connected with each other. Mental peace acts on the body and keeps it sound, as soundness of body strengthens the mind. Even in *yoga* there are two opinions on this subject. It is held that the breath (*prâṇa*) in the body is a part of the universal breath (*prâṇa*), and that health of mind and body, accompanied by spiritual bliss and knowledge, will ensue on controlling the individual (*piṇḍa* or *vyaṣṭi*) breath in such a manner as to attune it to the cosmic (*brahmâṇḍa* or *samaṣṭi*) breath. This principle in its enunciation is perfectly correct; but there are some who hold that this can be accomplished by regulating the breath (*prâṇâyâma*, *pratyâhâra*, etc.), because *vṛtti* always follows *prâṇa*. These are called *haṭha-yogins*, because they aim only at that union of *ha* (*prâṇa*) and *ṭha* (*apâna*) which leads to *samâdhi*. Their methods are therefore more physical than mental. There are, however, others who hold the contrary opinion, and address themselves principally to the work of *vṛttinirodha*, firmly believing that *prâṇa* follows *vṛtti*. This is *râja-yoga* (direct union with the Illustrious-soul or *Brahma*) the essence of the teachings of the unitary *Vedânta*. The *vedântic râjayoga* is the real *târaka-jñâna*, and indeed the word *râjayoga* is a synonym of *samâdhi*. The end proposed in *hatha-* as well as *râja-yoga* is the same, but the methods differ. *Vedântic rajayoga* aims at *sattvâ patti* and *vṛttinirodha*, but it aims at something beyond. It aims at that unity wherein every sense of separateness, impliedly present, in some form, in *vṛttinirodha* and *sattvâpatti*, is merged in the absolute bliss of One consciousness. The present age of physical science and corresponding mental development not accompanied by the necessary moral elevation can hardly appreciate the capabilities of *Yoga*, but the power of the mind and the will is a fact beyond dispute. Every act has its special condition, every rule its peculiar antecedents. Given the condition, the mind or rather the will can do anything, can call something out of nothing. Nothing is a misleading word, for nothing comes out of nothing; the Yoga believes that *prakṛiti* or matter is all full of life and it pervades everything and obeys the directions of a well-trained will. If we bear these considerations in mind, the principles of *Râja-Yoga* will appear more correct and more in accordance with natural truth than those of *Hatha-Yoga*.* The *Sutras* of Patanjali also lean more to the former than to the latter.

Two other kinds of *yoga* are often mentioned, but they are more or less included in the above. The first is *mantra-yoga* which consists in mentally repeating certain formulæ with intent contemplation of their meaning. This process is useful in every act of *hatha-* as well as *râja-yoga*. The second is *laya-yoga* which consists in intently contemplating any external object or, more properly, the internal *nâda* (sound) heard on closing the ears. This may be carried to the extent of *samâdhi*. Care, however, should be taken in all *yoga*-practices not to fall into the negative condition of passive mediumship, nor to lose the point in contemplation. This *laya-yoga* also is useful in all *Hatha-* and *Raja*-practices.

---

* For detailed particulars of Râjayoga the student may be referred to the second edition of my book of that name.

The *Yoga-sutras* are conveniently divided into four sections. The first deals with the meaning of *samâdhi* and *yoga*. The second points out those preliminary qualifications, both positive as well as negative, which a student must acquire. The third treats of *samâdhi*, its stages, and the powers consequent upon its acquisition. The fourth clearly explains the aim of the philosophy, *viz*, *kaivalya*. The student will be able to go through the following pages with some interest after these preliminary remarks.

THE YOGA-SUTRA.

SECTION I.

I. Now, an exposition of *Yoga* (is to be made).

The word 'now' indicates that a new topic commences at this point, and that the pupil is to attend to what follows. The *Sanskṛta* equivalent of it serves, by its mere repetition, for a benediction. This work is called an exposition, in as much as Patanjali is not the author of this system. He is only a compiler or explainer of the doctrine taught and practised of old by Hiraṇyagarbha and others. What is *Yoga?*

II. *Yoga* is the suppression of the transformations of the thinking principle.

The word *Yoga* has often been rendered by meditation or concentration, which both are not sufficient to convey the full import of the term. In order to explain the meaning it is necessary to understand what is the thinking principle, and what are its transformations. 'The thinking principle' is a comprehensive expression equal to the *Sanskṛta* word *Antaḥkaraṇa* which is divided* into four parts: *manas* (mind), the

* This division is after the *Vedánta* School and not the *Sánkhya* of which the *Yoga* is a complement, but all the same, it will do for all practical purposes.

principle which cognises generally; *Chitta* (individualising), the idea which fixes itself upon a point and makes the object its own by making it an individual; *Ahankâra* (egoism), the persuasion which connects the individual with the self; and *Buddhi* (reason), the light that determines one way or other. Knowledge or perception is a kind of transformation (*pariṇâma*) of the thinking principle into anything which is the subject of external or internal presentation, through one or other of these four. All knowledge is of the kind of transformations of the thinking principle. Even the Will which is the very first essential of *Yoga* is a kind of such transformation. *Yoga* is a complete suppression of the tendency of the thinking principle to transform itself into objects, thoughts, &c. It is possible that there should be degrees among these transformations, and the higher ones may assist to check the lower ones; but *Yoga* is acquired only when there is complete cessation of the one or the other, as will be seen later on. It should distinctly be borne in mind that the thinking principle is not the *A'tman*, the *Puruśa*, who is the source of all consciousness and knowledge. The suppression of the transformations of the thinking prinicple does not, therefore, mean that the *Yogin* is enjoined to become nil which certainly is impossible. This difficulty is touched upon in the next *sutra*. The thinking principle has three properties, *Sattva* (passivity), *Rajas* (restlessness) and *Tamas* (grossness). When the action of the last two is checked, the mind "stands steady like the jet of a lamp in a place protected from the smallest breeze."* It is such a condition of the internal sense that is most desirable as easily capable of being used for purposes of steady concentration, and absorbing application, as also for receiving the highest

---

* *Bhagvad-Gitâ*, ch. VI.

possible knowledge by free communion with nature, as Vâchaspatimiśra puts it.

III. Then the seer abides in himself.

Then, *i. e.*, at the time of *Yoga*. For if *Yoga* means complete suspension of the transformations of the thinking principle, what is it that the soul, here called the seer, perceives? That which takes different forms is not the real seer, it is only *vṛtti* or *khyâti*, whereas that which stands unchanged through the series of transformations which it witnesses, is the proper ultimate seer—the soul, *Puruśa*. So even seems the rule of the *Sânkhya*. *Darśana* (consciousness) is ever one. When all the *Vṛttis* or transformations of the thinking principle are suppressed, there remains only the never-changing eternal seer, *Puruśa*, in perfect *sattva*, being the only perceiver. The ultimate fact of consciousness is itself and nothing else. This unalloyed bliss is the proper state of the highest *Yoga* (called *Nirbijasamâdhi*). All misery arises from allowing the thinking principle to cover, or take the place of, this immutable source of bliss and knowledge, and then assume as many forms as objects presented to it, either within or without. This very point is carried further in the next *Sutra*.

IV. But otherwise (he) becomes assimilated with transformations.

Otherwise, *i. e.*, when *Yoga* is not acquired or reached. The thinking principle transforms itself into objective and subjective phenomena, and the immutable seer is for the time obscured by it, or, which is the same thing, is assimilated into it. It is only when the state of *Yoga* is reached that the consciousness becomes quite pure and ready to receive all knowledge, and all impressions, from any source whatever. If this state is to be acquired by suppressing the transformations of the thinking principle, it is necessary to understand what these transformations are.

V. The transformations are fivefold, and painful or not-painful.

The transformations of the thinking principle, though innumerable in themselves, are, for the sake of clearness, classified under five heads, which again are each subdivided into painful and not-painful. The painful are to be mastered by the not-painful, and these, in their turn, by *paravairâgya*, (absolute non-attachment). These are enumerated in the following *Sutra*.

VI. (They are) Right knowledge, wrong knowledge, fancy, sleep, and memory.

Right knowledge means such knowledge as is unquestionably reliable and true. Though the word *Pramáṇa* is often used in the sense of instrument of knowledge, it refers here rather to the result than to the act. Each of these terms are now defined.

VII. Right knowledge (is) direct cognition or inference or testimony.

The *Yoga* is at one with the *Sânkhya* in admitting only three sources of right knowledge. The *Nyâya* adds *Upamána* (analogy) to which the *Mimànsâ*, which is followed by the *Vedânta*, adds *Anupalabdhi* (non-presence) and *Arthâpatti* (implication). *Pratyakśa* or direct cognition is that knowledge which is produced by the direct contact of any of the senses with the object of knowledge. Inference is knowledge produced by a previous knowledge of the relation between a characteristic mark and the possessor of that mark. Testimony is knowledge produced from such words as are not untrustworthy on acccount of being false. The highest testimony is the *Veda* (*A'gama*), the word of the most reliable—*Iśwara.* All this knowledge is, as will be remembered, nothing more than different modifications of the thinking principle. The *Yoga* holds that all modifications having the form of a conviction are reducible to one of these three conditions.

VIII. Wrong knowledge is false conception of a thing whose real form does not correspond to that conception.

An illustration to the point will be mother-o'-pearl mistaken for silver, or a post mistaken for a man. Doubt also may be included in the definition of this class of knowledge. This kind of knowledge is of no use.

IX. Fancy is the notion called into being by mere words, having nothing to answer to it in reality.

Vikalpa which ordinarily means doubt or option, is here meant to imply mere fancy. A notion which is nothing more than mere words, which in fact has nothing corresponding to it in nature, is called fancy; *e. g.*, the horns of a hare, the rising or setting of the sun, the thinking of the soul,* &c.

---

* The soul itself is nothing beyond thinking, *i. e.*, consciousness.

These illustrations clearly define *Vikalpa* to be something quite different from *Viparyaya* (Aph. VIII.)

X. That transformation which has nothingness for its basis is sleep.

That is to say, sleep is produced when all transformations of the thinking principle are reduced to nothing. This dreamless sleep is, then, as it were, a state of no-transformation; but it should not be understood that it is no transformation of the thinking principle. If it were so, the remembrance in the form 'I slept sound' would not follow on waking, for we never remember what we have not experienced. Again it is exactly because that this state is a transformation that it differs from *Samâdhi* (concentration) which is pure cessation of all transformation.

XI. Memory is the not-allowing a thing cognised to escape.

Knowledge produced by recollecting impressions of past experience is memory. This is the definition of memory generally adopted, and it appears to go in with what is laid down in the aphorism.

It may be remarked that of these five transformations of the thinking principle, right knowledge, wrong knowledge, and fancy belong to the waking state. When any of these become perceptible in sleep, it is dream. Sleep itself has no cognition whatever. Memory, however, may be of any of the five.

Having explained these transformations of the thinking principle, the author next considers the means of suppressing them.

XII. Its suppresion is secured by application and non-attachment.

Its, *i.e.*, of these transformations of the thinking principle. *Samâdhi* or complete suppression of the transformations of the mind is secured only by sustained application and non-attachment. It has been thought proper to translate the word *Vairâgya* by non-attachment rather than by the word dispossession as is usually done. That which attracts the mind and makes it assume various forms as passions, emotions, sensations, &c., is nothing but *râga*, attachment; and *Vairâgya*, therefore, is more the absence of all attachment than the absence of any single result of such attachment, as passion, &c.

XIII. Application is the effort towards the state.

Sthiti or state is that state in which the thinking principle, as it were, stands, unmoved and unmodified, like the jet of a lamp in a place not exposed to the wind. The steady, sustained effort to attain this *Sthiti* is called application.

XIV. It becomes a position of firmness, being practised for a long time, without intermission, and perfect devotion.

Application ripens into confirmed habit which is second nature. The way to render such application second nature is plain enough. The point is that the mind comes at an advanced stage to a position in which, though apparently performing the ordinary functions of life, it is really at rest. This is the real state of *Yoga* or *Samâdhi* and not, as is asserted by some, the power to recall the mind to itself at any given moment. It is said in almost all works on *Yoga* and *Vedânta* that real concentration is that in which the mind, wherever it is directed, is ever at rest.* To make this state second nature is the result of constant, steady application.

XV. The consciousness of having mastered (every desire) in the case of one who does not thirst for objects perceptible or scriptural, is non-attachment.

Perpceptible objects are objects of this world, or such as are within mortal knowledge. Scriptural are those that are mainly heard of in the scriptures and similar books. The former word includes all temporal goods, the latter spiritual, such as secret powers, attainment of heaven, &c. Real non-attachment means cessation of even the slightest desire for any of these things. The value of virtue is generally the sacrifice made for it, and the text, therefore, well remarks that non-attachment must be of the form of a consciousness of having withstood temptation; for, otherwise, there would hardly be any difference between stolidity and sense. It is only when the mind reaches this condition of freedom from attachment, that true knowledge begins to dawn upon it, as right reflection in a mirror cleared of dirt. Non-attachment is indeed the preliminary of real intuitional knowledge; and it is possible to secure it by "application."

XVI. That is the highest, wherein, from being the *Puruśa*, there is entire cessation of any, the least, desire for the *Guṇas*.

The *Guṇas* or properties of *Prakṛti* are well-known. That non-attachment, in which there is entire absense of the consciousness

* *Vákyasudhá.*

of having arrived at the state of the highest knowledge, is the greatest and best. The non-attachment described in the previous aphorism is followed by the rise of conscious intuitional knowledge (*Sattvaguṇa*); but the one intended here is not apart from what is called *Kaivalya* or final beatitude, wherein *all is Puruśa*, nothing exists besides *Puruśa*, the one life of all, ever unchangeable and purely blissful. This kind of *Vairâgya* is called *para* or the highest as distinguished from the former which is only *apara* or lower.

XVII. Conscious is that which is attended by argumentation, deliberation, joy, and the sense of being.

Here is described the state called *Samâdhi* or concentration, the end and aim of *Yoga*. It is of two kinds. The first is that in which there is consciousness of the thinker and the thought being apart. The second which will be just described takes no cognisance of such distinctions. Though the mind is free from transformations, still it is conscious of that which it identifies itself with, and hence this *Samâdhi* is called conscious (*Samprajnâta*) or with seed (*Sabija*).* *Samâdhi* is a kind of *Bhâvanâ*, *i. e.*, pondering on, or, becoming something.

The objects to meditate upon are none other than the 25 explained in the *Sânkhya*, and God, added to them by this School. Of these 25 categories or *Tattvas*, 24 are the products of *Prakṛti*, senseless matter, the 25th being the only category with sense, *viz.*, *Puruśa* or soul. When pondering is carried on with reference to the five gross elements and the organs of external

---

* It is called *Savikalpa* also.

perception, by way of ascertaining the relations of all these and of the names to their real sense, it is *Savitarka* or argumentative meditation. The same made the object of meditation without any argument as to their nature, relation, &c., is called *Nirvitarka* or non-argumentative meditation. When the five *Tanmâtras,* the subtile cause of the elements, and the internal organ of perception, are made the objects of meditation in relation to space, time, &c., it is *Savichâra* or deliberative meditation. The same thought of without any relation is *Nirvichârasamâdhi.* These two, with their opposites, are called *Grâhya-samâpatti*, the cognition of things cognisable.

When the quality of passivity (*Sattva*) is pondered upon, in the internal organ of perception, to the subordination of the other two, restlessness (*Rajas*) and grossness (*Tamas*), it is *Sânanda* or joyous meditation, for joy, the result of *Sattva,* the cause that enables the senses to perform their functions, is then experienced to its full. This is called *Grahaṇa-Samâpatti*, the cognition of the instrument of cognition. Those who stop at this stage and do not reach the *Puruśa* are called *Videha,* free from the bonds of matter. That wherein pure *Sattva* (passivity) alone is pondered upon, without the faintest colour of the other two, is called *Sâsmita,* or meditation with the sense of being. *Asmi* means I am, and *Asmita* is the sense of being. It is not egoism (*Ahankâra*), for here there is only the consciousness of being, independent of the form "I am." The sphere of *Ahankâra* is *Sânand Samâdhi,* whereas this refers, very nearly, to the *Puruśa* through and of which all subsists. This is called *Gṛhitṛ-Samâpatti*, the cognition of the knower. One who has reached this stage is called

Prakṛtilaya, i. e., one dissolved in *Prakṛti*, one who has not risen beyond it.*

In every act of pondering there is the knower, the known, and the instruments. The fourth kind of *Samâdhi* has reference only to the knower (*Gṛhitṛ*); the third to the instruments (*Grahaṇa, viz., the Indriyas*); and the first and second to the known, *i. e.*, objects (*Grâhya*). The first relates to the *Sthulabhutas* and *Indriyas;* the second to the *Tanmâtras* and *Antahkaraṇa*; the third to *Ahankâra*; and the fourth to *Puruśa*. To put it otherwise, meditation on some gross object as an idol or the form of some god, &c., is the first; meditation on the subtile cause of the gross form is the second; meditation on the instruments of knowledge and the cause that moves them is the third; and meditation of the cause of all causes, the real substratum of all, is the last. The first consists of all four; and the way to pass from the first to the second and onward is by excluding or ignoring such parts as are perfectly fixed in the mind, and are not likely to recur and interrupt further meditation.†

XVIII. The other is that which consists only of *Samskâras*, being brought on by the practice of the cause of complete suspension.

In interpreting this *Sutra* commentators are not at one. We follow the *Bhâśya* and *Vâchaspati*, rejecting *Bhoja*. We have the *Maṇiprabhâ* with us. The other means the other kind of

* *Vide* the Maṇiprabhâ. The meaning assigned to this word by Bhoja conflicts with his own explanation of the same under XVIII.

† For further elucidation *vide* Madhusudana in his commentary on the Bhagvad-Gitâ, chap. VI, verse 15.

Samâdhi—the *Asamprajnâta* or unconscious. In this concentration which is the proper aim of *Yoga* there is no particular consciousness of the knower or the known. It is brought about by the practice of that *Vairâgya* which is called *Para* (vide XVI), which is the cause of bringing the mind to a state of complete rest—a state in which all transformations are suspended or ended. The constant practice of this supreme non-attachment frees the mind even from the impression left upon it by the kind of *Samâdhi* described in the previous section, and fixes upon it its own stamp, and holds it in permanent equilibrium. *Samskâra* means impression, the mark left upon something by another thing—a mark which can at any time be called to life. Now, when supreme non-attachment sets its mark upon the mind and obliterates all previous impressions, it is plain that the mind having no other impression but that of *paravairâgya* to disturb it, if disturbance it can be called, must, of necessity, remain in a state of perfect equilibrium bordering upon vacuity, and yet indescribably blissful. This state is the state of perfect 'suspension of transformations,' (vide II) which is real *Yoga*. This unconscious meditation, *i. e.*, meditation in which there is no definite consciousness, is called *Nirbija*, void of seed, also.* *Samprajnâta-sâmdhi*, though good for practice, is of no use; for real *Yoga* consits, not in that kind of concentration, but in *asamprajnâta-samâdhi*, as will be seen.

XIX. Of those who are *Videha* and *Prakṛtilaya* the concrete universe is the cause.

Videha and *Prakṛtilaya* are explained under XVII. Those

---

* Also *Nirvikalpa*.

who have stopped only at that stage in progress are inferior *Yogins*, and their *Samâdhi* is only an inferior exercise ever dependent on the existence of the world. They are not cognisant of the ultimate reality, and are, therefore, immersed in the phenomenal world in which they are born and re-born, in one form or another, never mind even if after long intervals. It is said in the *Vâyupurâṇa*, "meditators on the *Indriyas* remain (in heaven) for 10 *Manvantaras* ; on the *Bhutâs* for a hundred ; on *Ahankâra* for a thousand ; on *Buddhi* for ten thousand ; on *Avyakta* for a lakh ; but the limit of time in the case of those who meditate on the *Parapuruśa* cannot be defined." Their ken is bounded by the material world, and this *Samâdhi* is, therefore, not the last and best end ; though it is useful as a means. Seekers after occult powers ought to lay these wise words of the sage Patanjali close to their heart. Proper *Samâdhi* does not care for the state of the one or the other.

XX. In others (it) is preceded by faith, energy, memory, descrimination.

It, that is, *Samâdhi*. *Samâdhi* in the case of true *Yogins* is preceded, not by the state of mere *Videha* or *Prakṛtilaya*, but by Faith, &c. Faith is the firm and pleasant conviction of the mind as regards the efficacy of *Yoga*. True faith always leads to energetic action, which again, by the potency of its vividness, calls to mind all previous knowledge of the subject. This is energy, which leads to proper discrimination of right and wrong. Those who apply themselves to *Yoga* with faith, &c., reach the highest *Samâdhi* through *Samprajnâta* which leads to *Paravairâgya* and then to *Asamprajnâta*.

XXI. (It is) nearest to those whose feeling is most ardent.

It is difficult to render the word *Samvega* into English. It is not only feeling, but a resolute influence over the mind which makes the whole soul one sentiment, and leads to immediate action. Commentators render it by the word *Vairâgya* which is the most approximate approach to its true sense. Those who feel ardently, *i. e.*, those whose *Vairâgya* is sufficiently keen, attain at once to the state of *Asamprajnâta-Samâdhi*.

XXII. A further distinction arises on account of mild, moderate, and excessive.

Mild, moderate, and excessive refer to the means mentioned under XVIII and XX. The means to attain the end must be mild, moderate, or excessive, but the *Tivrasamvega*, ardent feeling of non-attachment, should pervade them all. This *Samvega* also may be threefold, as mild, moderate, or excessive. Hence there would naturally be nine classes of *Yogins* ; for each of the *Yogins* with mild, moderate, or excessive means, will again be of mild, moderate, or excessive feeling. The result, unconscious concentration, will be proportionate to the degree of means and feeling.

XXIII. Or by devotion to *Iśvara*.

The attainment of *Parasamâdhi*, or unconscious concentration, is shown to be possible by another method. This is suggested by the particle 'or.' *Iśvara* is a word derived from the root *iś* to rule and means the supreme ruler. The nature of this *Iśvara* will be explained in the next aphorism.

Devotion means not only mental submission, but entire dependence or self-abandonment. The point is this. The main obstacle in the way of *Samâdhi* is attachment (*râga*), which causes transformations of the thinking principle. Now this *râga* arises only because we believe ourselves powerful to secure good and escape evil. If this false belief be abandoned, pure non-attachment, the nearest way to *Samâdhi*, will be the result. So long as this non-attachment can be brought about by the methods indicated, well and good; but when nothing succeeds, the way pointed out here will be found useful. One should so abandon himself to the will of the supreme that he must move about only to fulfil his benign wish, not to accomplish this or that result. He must bear all, good, bad, or indifferent, simply as an act of His grace, in carrying which out he pleases Him. The firm conviction that action is his lot, independent of the result whatever it be, is true devotion to *Iśvara*, and the way to *Paravairâgya*, the door of *Samâdhi*.

XXIV. *Iśvara* is a particular soul untouched by affliction, works, fruition, and impressions.

It is well known that the *Sânkhya* of which the *Yoga* is a complement recognises no *Iśvara*, for Kapila definitely says that his existence is "not proved." Patanjali puts in an *Iśvara* more for purposes of meditation and other subordinate conveniences than for any cardinal important purpose. His philosophy derives the name of *Seśvarasânkhya* from this circumstance. *Iśvara* is neither a personal being nor yet quite impersonal like the *Vedântic Brahma*. He is evidently a *Puruśa* and a particular *Puruśa* inasmuch as he is unlike the known or knowable *Puruśas*. He is ever free, ever absolved, ever omniscient. He is untouched, at *any* period of time, for otherwise even *Muktas*, those who are absolved, will be included in the term, by afflictions, works, fruition, and impression. They will all be defined later on, but it may here be remarked that it is exactly these things which, according to this philosophy, are the cause of this unhappy existence, freedom from which is the aim of *Yoga*. *Iśvara*, the final resort of beings, must evidently be free from these.

XXV. In him is the highest limit of the seed of omniscience.

As every quality is seen to attain its limit in no limit, so also does omniscience, a quality of the *Antahkaraṇa*. He in whom omniscience is developed to this point can be none other than *Iśvara*. This aphorism, though describing a particular quality of the godhead, gives no clear proof for such assumption; and is thus not of much use in rendering Patanjal's idea of God quite definite. It would not perhaps be quite apart from his view even if we held that this *Iśvara* is the all-pervading spirit manifest in nature.

XXVI. Being unconditioned by time he is the greatest of the great.

This requires no explanation. Omniscience must be undefined by time, and hence He whose knowledge and existence are not limited is the greatest of all conceivable entities, whether gods, worlds, or creations.

XXVII. His indicator is the "word of glory."

The "word of glory" is the *Praṇava* which literally means that which glorifies well. This is the mystic word OM, the very essence of all teaching. As to its proper meaning the best concise explanation may be seen in the *Mândukya-Upaniśad.* All sacred books from the Veda to the *Purâṇa* teach that this mystic syllable is the secret of secrets and the source of all power. It is said to be the indicator of *Iśvara* not because like ordinary words it is conventionally used by men in that sense, but because it itself is *Iśvara*, its very form has that truth embodied in it, which is the essence of the universe in its evolved, as well as involved, condition.

XXVIII. Its constant repetition, and intent meditation on its meaning, (should be practised).

Japa means repetition, but it should be accompanied by proper meditation on the meaning of the words or syllables repeated. The best way of such repeating recommended by the *Tantras* is *Mânasa, i. e.,* mental, such that it never ceases even during work, nay, even in sleep.

XXIX. Thence arises cognition of the subjective, and absence of obstacles.

The proper end to which the said *Japa* is a means is none other than *Samâdhi*; but the intermediate advantage of such practice is also indicated. *Pratyak* means that which "goes against" the ordinary tendency of the senses, which is always external. *Chetana* is none other than *puruśa*, the intelligence that is inseparable from nature. We call the being engrossed in the pure form of this intelligent consciousness 'cognition of the subjective' for want of a better expression. The meaning is plain enough, for it is implied that the senses cease to flow outside, and tend to the real inward source of all action and intelligence. It need not be doubted how repetition of the name of *Iśvara* leads to cognition of the subjective self for, in reality, both are one by their similiarity of attributes, says the *Maṇiprabhâ*. The next advantage is the absence of obstacles The next *sutra* proceeds to define the obstacles.

XXX. Disease, Dullness, Doubt, Carelessness, Sloth, Worldly-mindedness, False notion, Missing the point, and Instability, are the causes of distracting the mind, and they are the obstacles.

Disease, Dullness, Doubt, Carelessness, Sloth, are all plain enough. Worldly-mindedness is meant for that tendency of the mind which unceasingly yearns after one or other kind of momentary enjoyment; False notion is the being misled into believing some state other than the one desired, to be the desired one. Missing the point is going astray from the real point *viz., Samâdhi*. Instability is that fickleness of the mind which does not allow it to remain in the condition of *Samâdhi* even after it has reached it. These are the things which distract the mind and prevent it from being brought to a point; they are therefore called obstacles in the way of *Samâdhi*. These are never experienced by those who follow the method laid down in XXVIII.

XXXI. Pain, Despair, Nervousness, Inspiration, Expiration, are the accompaniments of the causes of distraction.

That is to say, these follow in the train of the obstacles enumerated in XXX. They are indicators of the state of the mind. Pain, despair, nervousness, are plain enough. So too are inspiration and expiration. But it is implied that when the mind is distracted inspiration and expiration are not in their normal condition. Abnormal state of breathing, as also any of the states described as pain, &c., are, therefore, a sure indication of distraction. The most proper state of the breath, indicative of entire calmness or real *Samâdhi*, is complete suspension accompanied with serene calmness of the mind.

XXXII. To prevent these (there should be) intense application to any one thing.

The mind must somehow be made steady. To this end *Samprajnâta-Samâdhi*, conscious meditation, must always and at every moment be practised. It may be practised by intense application to any one thing as shown under XVII. The *Bhâsya* here goes at great length to establish the unity of mental consciousness as against those Nihilists (*Bauddhas*) who maintain that all our knowledge is nothing but a bundle of varying momentary consciousnesses, so to speak, but the discussion is of no real importance to the subject in hand.

XXXIII. The mind (becomes) cheeful by the practice of sympathy, compassion, complacency, and indifference, respectively, towards happiness, misery, virtue, and vice.

Here is indicated the best and easy way of keeping the mind in that condition of evenness which is most favourable to *Samâdhi*. Sympathy here refers to that identity of feeling with the object of the emotion which one experiences on seeing happiness or misery. If we see one happy our feeling also must be identical; this is sympathy. Compassion is the same feeling for misery of whatever kind ; but it should be borne in mind that mere passive sentiment is not what is meant. It inplies as much action on the part of him who feels the emotion as lies in his power. Complacency is joy at the sight of virtue and the sacrifices incidental to its practice. As to vice and folly which unfortunately enter by far too largely in the composition of "the world" the least that one should do is entire indifference. If he can help to cure the one and remove the other it is sacrifice of a superior kind ; but for one whose end and aim is nothing but *Samâdhi*, indifference is the best attitude to maintain.

XXXIV. Or by the expiration and retention of the breath.

This aphorism suggests another method of steadying the mind. Patanjali takes it for granted that the reader is acqainted with what is called *Prâṇâyâma*, a word sometimes used collectively for the inhaling, retention, and exhaling, of the breath, and sometimes for each of these severally. It means "restraining the breath." Even the order is not certain. Some would take it in the order of exhaling, inhaling, and retaining; others of inhaling, retaining, and exhaling. Patanjali refers only to exhaling and retention, but as retention is not supposed to be possible without inhaling, several commentators have thought it necessary to understand the order as exhaling, inhaling, and retention, followed again by exhaling, &c. The *Maṇiprabhâ*, however, suggests that the breath may be sent out and the retention would then consist in merely not allowing any new air to enter the nostrils. For a clear analysis of this very extensive and important subject the student ought to consult the *Hathapradipikâ* or any similar work.—(*Vide* Appendix.)

XXXV. Or engrossing cognition of any sensuous enjoyment, brought about, is the cause of steadying the mind.

Another mode of steadying the mind in the case of those who cannot do so but through some kind of sensual pleasure is fixing the attention on one of the five senses of smell, taste, colour, touch, and sound. These are respectively produced by concentrating on the tip of the nose, the tip of the tongue, the forepart of the palate, the middle of the tongue, and the roof of the tongue. The sensation produced in each case is not merely a passing flash of pleasurable feeling, but a kind of complete absorption in the particular enjoyment totally meditated upon. It should never be forgotten that this is only a means to the end.

XXXVI. Or that sorrowless condition of the mind, full of light (would conduce to *SamÂdhi.*)

The light here referred to is the light of pure *Sattva.* When the mind is deeply absorbed in that quality, then, indeed, does this condition of light which is free from all pain follow. Vachaspatimi'sra remarks that in the heart there is a lotus-like form having eight petals and with its face turned downward. One should raise this up by *Rechaka* (exhalation of the breath) and then meditate upon it, locating therein the four parts of the *praṇava*, viz., *a*, *u*, *m*, and the point, in their several meanings. When the mind thus meditating falls in the way of the *Suśumṇâ*, it sees a perfect calm light like that of the moon or the sun, resembling the calm ocean of milk. This is the *Jyotis*, light, which is the sure sign of complete *Sattva*. Some such practice is here meant.

XXXVII. Or the mind intent upon those free from attachment, &c., (will lead to the end.)

Vitarâgas, those free from attachment, the result of *Rajas* (restlessness) and *Tamas* (grossness), and the cause of all woe, are things or persons full of *Sattva* (passivity) alone. Such persons are great Mahâtmâs like Krisṇadvaipàyana, *S'*uka, Sanaka, and others. Ráma, S'iva, Kṛsṇa, Christ, Buddha, or even any imaginary entity answering to the requisite quality will do, according to ones predilection. The point is that the absorption of the mind in another mind ever steady and blissful will produce a corresponding effect and lead to *Samâdhi*.

XXXVIII. Or depending on the experience of dream and sleep (will lead to the result).

The *Yoga* does not regard sleep as mere blank; and hence the recommendation to concentrate the mind on the condition of deep sleep. Dream is that condition of the mind wherein it alone is active to the exclusion of the external senses. Even this condition is a fit object to concentrate upon for the end in view. It will be useful in training the imagination, which is the first step towards *Samâdhi*.

XXXIX. Or by meditating according to one's predilection.

Having suggested so many methods of steadying the mind, Patanjali gives the principle underlying all of them in one word. It is only necessary to habituate the mind to remain absorbed in, or to call to life, any thing for, and at a given time; it is a matter of indifference what the thing is and how the habit is acquired. The careful reader will, however, easily see from the foregoing methods that objects of sense, and things that easily excite, or are in any way connected with bad associations and influences, are not recommended as fit objects to concentrate upon.

XL. His mastery extends from the finest atom to infinity.

The test of proper concentration having been acquired is mastery commencing from over the smallest of atoms to the most inconceivable magnitude—infinity. One who is able to identify his mind with the object meditated upon, in fact to lose himself in the object, can accomplish this.

XLI. In the case of one the transformations of whose mind have been annihilated, there is entire identity with, and complete absorption in, the cogniser, the cognition, and the cognised, like a transparent jewel.

The way in which the mind of a real *Yogin* acquires mastery over nature is here described. When the mind is brought to a point by the suspension of its transforming tendencies, it is as colourless as a piece of pure rock-crystal, and just becomes what it stands upon. This is explained by saying that there is complete identity with, and absorption in, the object thought of. The mind in fact loses itself in the object meditated upon, and that object is the only thing which is seen in its place, as in the case of the crystal placed upon any colour. All things in the universe can be classed under three heads in relation to the cognising mind, *viz.*, things cognised, the instrument of cognition, and the cogniser. The mind becomes any of these as it meditates upon them. It may be marked that the order of the three is not properly given in the text. The explanation thus given must enable one to understand how a *Yogin* can by mere act of concentration *accomplish anything.*

XLII. The argumentative condition (of the concentrated mind) is that which is mixed with thoughts of word, meaning, and understanding.

Having finished the description of conscious *Samâdhi*, the author again reverts to the subject of its divisions. He divides this kind of *Samâdhi* into two kinds: *Sthula* or gross, *i. e.*, relating to the *Bhutas*; and *Sukśma* or subtile, *i. e.*, relating to the *Tanmâtras* and *Indriyas* (vide XVII). This and the following *Sutra* refer to the *Sthula* or gross division of *Samprâjnata-Samâdhi.* Every thing has a name which bears some meaning, and the relation of the object and its name is understood in some way. When the mind apprehends a word and meditates upon its meaning and form, as also upon the understanding of either, and thus loses itself in the thing, in the manner described in XLI, it is called *Savitarka-Samâdhi.*

XLIII. Non-argumentative is that in which the meaning alone is present, as if quite unlike itself, on memory being dissolved.

The meaning is that when everything besides the perfect idea of the object meditated upon is forgotten it is *Nirvitarka-Samâdhi.* When the mind is not conscious of name, form, meaning, or relation; when, in fact, the object has, as it were, destroyed itself by its real nature, as understood through name, &c., being absent, there follows complete absorption in some one *idea* which prevails. This is brought about by a suppression of the faculty of memory which generally associates ideas to their names, &c. This state is complete non-argumentative *Samâdhi*.

XLIV. By these, the deliberative and non-deliberative having reference to the subtile elements are also explained.

Just as the two kinds of argumentative concentration refers to the gross elements, so the two kinds of deliberative concentration refers to the subtile elements. These include the other two: *sânanda* and *sâsmita*.

XLV. The province of the subtile ends with the indissoluble.

The indissoluble is *Alinga*, that which cannot be resolved into anything else, says the *Bhâśya*. The *Sânkhya*-classification of elements may be divided from the stand-point of the resolvability of one into the other into four groups: gross (*i. e., the Bhutas*), subtile (*i. e.*, the *Tanmâtras* and *Indriyas*), intelligent (*i. e.*, *mahat*), and the indissoluble (*i. e.*, *Pradhâna*). It should be remarked that as we go higher we ascend in subtility or indissolubility. Though there is the *Puruśa* more subtile than *Pradhâna*, still, as it is not its *cause*, *Pradhâna* is the final point in the series of groups resolvable into one another. One who has mastered the said four stages of concentration obtains mastery over *Pradhâna*, and his power therefore extends up to that which is the very essence of Nature. The four stages here discussed ought to be understood as including the two other *Samprajnâta-Samâdhis*, *viz.*,

Sânanda and *Sâsmita*, for they have reference to the same group of objects and elements. Each of these also may be divided into *Savikalpa* and *Nirvikalpa* and the kinds of conscious *Samâdhi* may therefore be considered eight in all.

XLVI. These constitute seeded-meditation.

The meaning is plain. Inasmuch as there is conciousness in this kind of *Samâdhi* it is called seeded, for there is the seed which, on waking, may grow into various distractions from the condition of Samâdhi.

XLVII. The purity of the non-deliberative being reached, internal contentment follows.

The last stage of *samâdhi* developes a sense of complete intellectuality, or complete absorption in the soul. This leads to permanent joy and contentment. This is called *Adhyâtmaprasâda.* The qualities of *rajas* and *tamas* being entirely annihilated, so to speak, and *sattva* alone remaining, there follows perfect light and purity which is the result of the predominance of *sattva.* Suspension of transformation leads to the condition of pure *sattva,* wherein alone it is possible to experience the bliss consequent upon true recognition of the *puruśa.* The *purusá* which is all bliss, all knowledge, and ever free, is then seen and experienced in his true character. This is *prasâda,* the joyous, contented state of the mind.

XLVIII. The intellect is there truth-bearing.

All that interferes with a true intuitive recognition of nature, being removed, truth, as it were, flows in towards the point which is thus prepared to receive it. The intellect receives real knowledge by mere intuition in this condition.

XLIX. Its subject is different from that of revelation and inference, for it refers to particulars.

The instruments of knowledge, as it will be remembered, are three, *viz.*, direct cognition, inference, testimony (*i.e.*, revelation, the highest testimony). The knowledge which arises in this condition is of the first order, and superior to that which arises from the other two. Revelation and inference deal only with generalisations, and the latter is still further limited by referring only to what is actually accessible to the senses. Knowledge that intuitively springs up in the state of *Nirvichârasamâdhi* refers to the minutest particulars and is independent of time and place. It is evident that this kind of knowledge, though belonging to the class of *pratyakśa* (direct cognition), is yet different from it, inasmuch as it refers not to the general marks (*Jâti*) through which objects are generally cognised, but to the particular objects possessing the mark. The knowledge which is here implied is independent of connotation and denotation, and is therefore superior to all. That it is strictly true and always free from error requires no mentioning.

L. The impression thereof stands in the way of other impressions.

The impression on the mind produced by this *Samâdhi* prevents other impressions from gaining ground on it, and we know that the last truth impressed on the mind is none other than blissful cognition of the *Puruśa*. The mind ceases to transform itself into any thing besides this impression. The one great advantage of this *Samâdhi* is that the mind becomes free from all foulness and becomes so pure as to take to nothing but this *Samâdhi.*

LI. The prevention of that even, leads to the prevention of all, and thus to meditation without seed.

This has been partially explained under XVIII. The last impression which *Sabijasamâdhi* leaves must be obliterated by that kind of meditation which results from *Paravairâgya*, supreme non-attachment, and is of the form of "not-this, not-that," &c. The mind thus having nothing to rest upon exhausts itself to death, and *Puruśa* alone shines in perfect bliss and peace.

THE YOGA-SUTRA.

SECTION II.

I. Preliminary *Yoga* (consists of) mortification, study, and resignation to *Iśvara*.

The first section deals with *Samâdhi* and its character; the present one is meant for those who have not been able to accomplish that, or are not in that condition. As this section deals, therefore, with rules for the guidance of such students, it is aptly called *Kriyâyoga* or preliminary *Yoga.** By mortification is meant all those fasts, penances, observances, &c., which are laid down in the *Dharma-śâstras.* Study means the repetition of the *praṇava* or any holy *mantra* in the manner described before (XXVIII., Sect. I.), or the constant close reading of religious books bearing on them. Resignation to *Iśvara* has been fully described before (XXIII., Sect. I.) These then constitute the whole of the preliminary side of *Yoga*, and are sufficient, if carefully and sincerely practised, to lead to *Samâdhi*.

II. (They are practised) for acquiring habitual *Samâdhi*, and for attenuating distractions.

The usefulness of preliminary *Yoga* is here described. It leads the mind into a constant habit of *Samâdhi*, by first

* The expression practical Yoga is obviously misleading, and is therefore rejected.

attenuating those causes which distract the mind and then by completely destroying them.

III. The distractions are five, *viz.*, Ignorance, the Sense of being, Desire, Aversion, and Attachment.

These will be defined.

IV. Ignorance is the source of those that follow, whether they be in the dormant, attenuated, overpowered, or expanded condition.

Though the causes of distraction are five in number, they all arise from ignorance which, therefore, is the real great distraction. All distraction is misery. Distractions, *i.e.*, their causes, are here shown to be of four kinds. They may be dormant, that is, not developed for want of proper conditions, as in the case of those who are described as *Videha* and *Prakṛtilaya* (XIX., Sect. I). It is for this reason that they are not really *mukta*, absolved. Attenuated as in the case of those devoted to preliminary *Yoga*. The force of the causes of distraction is reduced to its lowest minimum, and hence they disturb them but seldom. Overpowered and expanded are in the case of those who are in the ordinary course of life. These are only relative terms, for the distractions are overpowered, *i. e.*, held in suspension, for a time, when a contrary impulse is expanded, and *vice versa*. An example in point is that of a man who loves an object with which he loses his temper for a moment. The love is at first expanded and becomes overpowered when anger takes its place. Over and above these four conditions of the causes of distraction, a fifth must be taken notice of, though, being the same as

Samâdhi, it need not constitute itself into a separate class. Those whose distractions are reduced to zero, are those who are in *Samâdhi*; and it should not be forgotten that this is the real condition to which these distractions must be reduced before aspiring to *Samâdhi*. Preliminary *Yoga* will be a help of no mean importance.

V. Ignorance is taking the non-eternal, impure, evil, and non-*âtmâ*, to be eternal, pure, good, and *âtmâ*.

The shortest explanation of ignorance is taking a thing for what it is not. It should, however, be remarked that it does not imply mere privation of knowledge as the word *Avidyâ* may suggest. It is a positive mental state which induces the result of taking a thing for what it is not. It is neither one of the instruments of knowledge (*pramâṇa*), nor an absence of them, but a something apart from them all. When there is no *avidyâ*, the instruments of knowledge, the thing to be cognised, and all similar distractions, are reduced to naught, and one sole unity, all knowledge and bliss, is the result. Hence it is easy to see that ignorance is neither one of the instruments of knowledge nor apart from them, but it is in fact that thing by which the original unit appears threefold, as the cogniser, the cognised, and the instrument of cognition.

VI. The Sense of being is the blending together of the power that knows with the instruments thereof.

It is well known that the ultimate source of knowledge, the real seer, is the *puruśa* within. When the instruments through which the *puruśa* sees, such as the mind or the senses through which the mind works, are identified with the *puruśa*, and all is seen as if blended in one, this process is called the Sense of being. When by the force of ignorance the internal "I," as it were, becomes assimilated with external objects, there arises this feeling, the cause of all pain and distraction. The full import will be clear under aphorisms XVII.—XXIII.

VII. That which dwells on pleasure is Desire.

VIII. That which dwells on pain is Aversion.

The meaning of these two aphorisms is plain.

IX. The strong desire for life, seen even in the learned, and ever sustained by its own force, is Attachment.

Desire for life is indeed the cause of attachment of every description, and the real cause at the bottom of every misery of which the world is full. It is a feeling from which none is free, from the lowest worm to the highest sage; nay even so-called inanimate nature is not free from it. It is not produced in beings, by education or example, but is purely innate; and the very child is as much full of it as the man bending down with age. Hence it is inferred that every being brings this feeling with it at birth from the experiences of its previous life, of which this feeling is thus an indirect proof, and thus the current of this 'desire for life' begins only in eternity. It is, therefore, well said that it is ever sustained by its own force. The desire for life is the cause of fear, in thousand forms, and is well typified by popular mystical writers by the dreadful "Dweller-on-the-Threshold," the enemy of all who aspire after secret knowledge.

The five distractions are called by other names also. Ignorance *(avidyâ)* is called darkness *(tamas)*, being the cognition of soul in those that are not-soul, viz., the five *Tanmâtras*, *Mahat*, *Ahankâra*, and *Avyakta*. The second, egoism (*asmitâ*), is called delusion *(moha)*, being the identifying of the *Yogin's* self with the form he takes by the secret powers *(siddhis)* acquired, such as atomic, ethereal, &c. The third, desire *(râga)*, is called great delusion (*mahâmoha*), being the losing oneself in the pleasures of the higher objects for the finest sensual pleasures, through sound, taste, &c. The fourth, aversion *(dveśa)*, is called obscuration *(tâmisra)*, being great disgust felt for the obscurations in the way of complete enjoyment of *iśatva*, mastery over *all*. The last, attachment (*abhiniveśa*), is called blindfoldedness *(andhatâmisra)*, being the fear that the powers acquired will be lost. This description is briefly inserted in this place only to show that even after the greatest occult powers are acquired, the five distractions do not quite leave the *Yogin*, and he is therefore as far away from real *mokśa* as he ever was.

X. These, the subtile ones, must be suppressed by a contrary course.

Having described the nature of distractions, the author points out the way to suppress them. They are divided into two kinds, subtile and gross. The first are those which exist in a dormant condition in the form of impressions, whereas the second are those that appear in concretely affecting the mind. The first can be completely suppressed only by gaining mastery over the whole of their support, *viz.*, the thinking principle; and the way pointed out in the text suggests that course. The subtile distractions must be suppressed by a course contrary to their existence, and this course, in the case of their seed-like existence, is none other than the merging of the mind in the pure sense of being, in *Prakṛti*, the root of all.

XI. Their transformations are to be suppressed by meditation.

The other kind of distractions, *viz.*, the gross ones are seen by their results, *viz.*, the transformations of the thinking principle. These are to be suppressed by meditation as described in Sect. I; or by the means described at the beginning of this Section.

XII. The impressions of works have their root in distractions, and are experienced in the seen or the unseen.

Having described the distractions and the way of suppressing them, it is proposed to show why they are called distractions. They are called distractions, the cause of misery, for all *karmas* arise from them, and lead to happiness or misery. *Karma* or work, rather causes which govern the position of beings, begin in no beginning, and are continued by what are called impressions left by previous *karmas*, which impressions become ripe for fruition, either good or bad, when it is their time. The results of *karma* are experienced either in the seen, *i. e.*, in this very existence, or in the unseen, *i. e.*, in some other incarnation, in proportion to the effort put forth. It should, however, be borne in mind that in the case of those whose distractions are completely suppressed or destroyed the latter alternative does not hold true; for *karmas* have their root in distractions which being nowhere, *karmas* also become powerless for fruition. All *karmas* do not produce their results at once, nor does one *karma* succeed another, but the mysterious law works in some inscrutable manner, and such parts of the aggragate as are ripe for fruition, produce results under proper circumstances. The division of *karmas* into *sanchita*, *prârabdha*, *kriyamâṇa*, after the *Advaita* philosophy, is most important to explain, even approximately, the operations of this mysterious law of laws.*

XIII. The root being there, their fruition (consists in) class, life, and experience.

The root means the root in the form of distractions. If it is there the result of *karma* is sure to follow. Their, *i.e.*, of *karmas*. The result or fruition of *karma* consists in one of three things, or all of them, or any two of them, *viz.*, class, life, experience. The word class does not convey the whole import of the word *Jâti* which refers to rank, class, birth, or what are called orders and genera as well. The meaning, however, is plain enough. The being placed in one particular position is the result of *karma*. So is also the length or shortness of life ; and so also the pleasantness or otherwise of the experiences of a life-time. Hence the results of *karma* are threefold.

XIV. They have pleasure or pain for thier fruit according as their cause is virtue or vice.

They, *i. e.*, the three : class, life, and experience. The meaning is plain.

---

* Vide my "Monism or Advaitism ?"—Section *Karma*.

XV. To the enlightened *all* is *misery*, on account of consequences, anxiety, and impressions; as also on account of the opposition of the action of qualities.

To the enlightened, *i. e.*, to one who has made some progress in *Yoga*, and has thereby acquired that keen intuition which is able to distinguish at once between the eternal and the illusive. *All*, *i.e.*, every nameable thing, concrete or abstract, is not only full of misery, but is misery itself. Just as the eyeball cannot bear the touch of the finest thread of wool, which other parts of the body can hardly even feel, so even does one of refined intellect bear his connection with mundane things. It is to him all pain and misery, though the coarser part of humanity should take no notice of its character whatever. Four reasons are given to show how everything is full of misery. The first is consequences. Even when a thing, good, bad, or indifferent, is being experienced, that very experience creates a desire for more, and leads, on its non-fulfilment which is often most possible, to uneasiness, disappointment, and misery. The second is anxiety. The anxiety for retaining the objects of our love and pleasure, and for protecting them from interference, is infinitely great. The third is impression. Every experience leaves an impression which, though feeble and latent for the time, is sure, at its proper time, to awaken in full force and create a desire for enjoyment which, fulfilled or unfulfilled, is sure to lead to misery in the manner described above. Over and above these three, the one important cause is the natural opposition which exists between the individual actions of each of the three qualities. The result of passivity is pleasure and happiness, that of restlessness is disgust and misery, that of grossness is delusion. There is hardly any one thing which is not made up of these three qualities, as obviously there is nothing which is free from being the source of pleasure, pain, delusion, &c., at the same time, to different parties; and by turns, even to the same. Thus the enlightened must look upon everything as full of misery and free himself from contact.

XVI. That misery which is not yet come is to be warded off.

To be warded off is not an apt rendering of the *sanskṛta*—*heya*, which means both to be warded off, as well as possible to be warded off. That which is capable of being prevented, and should therefore be prevented is misery which has not yet come. And this for the very good reason that what is being experienced cannot be the subject of consideration, nor even that which is already past. As in therapeutics, the disease, its nature, convalescence, and its nature, are the four things to be mainly considered, so even here the thing to be warded off, the nature thereof, absolution, and its nature, including the means, are to be carefully investigated. In this order, therefore, the inquiry begins with this aphorism.

XVII. The cause of that which is to be warded off is the junction of the seer and the sight.

The seer is *puruṣa*, and sight is all that is seen through it, as also the instrument through which it is seen, *viz.*, *buddhi*, the result of *sattva*. *Buddhi* or intellect is very near *puruṣa* and is active on that his, though not exactly by him. The falsely uniting the one with the other by the impression that they are one and the same is the union implied in the aphorism. It is the cause of all misery. The argument may be axtended from *buddhi* to the senses, and thence to the objects cognised, and *prakṛti* the root of all. The meaning may be easily understood when it is said that the junction of the seer and sight is the cause of all misery. All bliss is of and in the *Puruṣa*, the seer, which is ever pure and free; and misery arises from confounding the *puruṣa* with objects which are not-*puruṣa*.

XVIII. The sight consists of the elements and the organs, is of the nature of illumination, action, and position, and is of use so far as experience and absolution are concerned.

It should be clearly borne in mind that the *Sânkhya*-theory of the universe is perfectly evolutional in its character, and that, therefore, everything is a direct or indirect *form* of the original *prakṛti*, which again is nothing different from "that wherein the three qualities are in a state of equilibrium"—*Triguṇasâmyâvasthâ*. The three *Guṇaṣ*, *Sattva*, *Rajas* and *Tamas*, have illumination, action, and mere position or the enduring or vegetating in a state of non-illumination, as their respective effects. These three being the source of everything we see, the whole universe can be nothing more nor less than a mere modification of them, and should exist in one or other of the three conditions. Hence the aphorism correctly observes that sight is of the nature of illumination, action, and position. The *Sânkhya*-order of evolution is well-known, and, therefore, the aphorism at once says that sight consists of, *i. e.*, exists in the form of, the five gross elements together with the *tanmâtras*; and the eleven organs—internal and external, together with *buddhi* and *ahankâra*. All this evolution of the primordial substance, in its many forms, and threefold conditions, is useful in helping us on to final absolution, by full experience of the pleasures and pains attendant on being entangled in it. It should be noted that He, that is, the real knower, is not in or of all this, and therefore it is he who realises himself, after proper knowledge. All this panorama of *prakṛti* is *for* the *puruṡa*, and therefore is but a means to the end. For *puruṡa* having been realised the action of *prakṛti* at once ceases. Thus evolution is in a sense *for* Him, as the *sânkyas* emphatically hold.

XIX. The stages of the *Guṇas* are the defined the undefined, the dissoluble, and the indissoluble.

The meaning will be plain if this aphorism is read in connection with aphorism XLV., Sect. I. The four stages are there described as the gross, the subtile, the intelligent, and the indissoluble.

XX. The seer is pure gnosis, and though pure (appears to) see through intellect.

The seer, *i. e.*, the *puruṡa*, is all *gnosis*, knowlege, or that which is the indescribable cause and essence of consciousness. He is not subject to the process of evolution and never mixes himself in the evolving side of nature,—its inseparable half, *prakṛti*. It is therefore pure. But, all the same, the work of seeing, understanding, goes on notwithstanding, and an explanation is made by saying that though ever pure it appears to cognise through the intellect which by its very vicinity takes the spark of life and performs all actions connected with cognition. Through intellect, the *puruṡa* appears as if seeing though really he never sees or does anything besides. It is ever unique, and all bliss.

XXI. The being of the sight is for him.

The word *âtmâ* used in the original where the aphorism runs "the *âtmâ* of the sight is for Him," has been made by some a ground for useless mystification, notwithstanding the clear explanation of almost all commentators that it means *svarupa* or (its) proper nature. The word 'being' expresses almost the whole of the idea. That the sight, *i. e.*, *prakṛti* and its forms appear to be, become presented as existing, is not on account of any purpose or cause inherent in it, but for the purpose of showing itself, as it were, to him, *i. e.*, the *puruśa* or soul, who, though ever in it, is not of it, nor the cause of putting it in action. That this action of *prakṛti* is on account of and for *puruśa* is beautifully described by a number of illustrations in works of *Sânkhya* philosophy. As milk which is not sentient flows of itself, in a sense by and necessarily for the calf, so indeed does *prakṛti* work by and for the *puruśa*—the seer, ever free and all bliss. If the *puruśa* were not, the being of *prakṛti* could never have been. The utility of *prakṛti* to the *puruśa* is already touched upon in aphorism XVIII.

XXII. It, though destroyed in the case of him whose purpose has been fulfilled, is yet not destroyed for it is common to others besides him.

The argument of the preceding aphorism is now carried to its logical issue. The *Sânkhya*-theory holds that though *prakṛti* or dead nature is only one, the inseparable *puruśas*, of and for which it exists, are many. Hence it is obvious that though the action of *prakṛti* should cease to affect such of the *puruśas* as have been able to realise themselves, the effects of its action on the rest of the *puruśas* must continue all the same. It, in the aphorism, means the sight, that is, *prakṛti.* This aphorism is intended as an answer to the objection that the absolution of one soul will imply the absolution of all, and hence an entire annihilation of *prakṛti* or nature which is eternal and indestructible.

XXIII. Junction is the cause of the self-recognition of its, as well as its lord's, power.

The junction of the seer and sight which is indicated as the thing to be warded off in aphorism XVII, is now clearly defined. It is evident from XXI. and XXII. that *puruśa*, the seer, and *prakṛti,* the sight, are in inseparable union from time without beginning. It is this junction that, while it is the cause of all experience, pleasurable or otherwise, is, at the same time, the cause of leading the *puruśa* to realise itself, *i. e.*, to *mokśa.* The very same thing is said in the *sutra* after its own peculiar phraseology. The power of it, *i. e.*, the sight or *prakṛti,* is that it appears, though dead, to exist, and produce experience (*bhoga*)of varied character. The power of its lord, *i. e.*, the seer or *puruśa*, through and of and for whom is its existence, consists in pure *gnosis* and bliss. That *prakṛti* should exist and *puruśa* should know itself, or in other words, that experience and absolution should arise, is dependent on the union of the two, commencing, it should be added, in time without beginning. He who understands the nature of this union and thus realises his (*puruśa's*) true nature is absolved. Hence this junction which leads to wrong knowledge, is put down as an evil to be warded off.

XXIV. Its cause is ignorance.

Its, *i. e.*, of the junction of the seer and the sight. Ignorance is defined under V.

XXV. The break of the junction, through the dispersion of ignorance, is the (thing) to be warded off; it is the *Kaivalya* of the Seer.

The break of the junction cannot be a physical break as is plain from XXIII. When ignorance is destroyed by right knowledge, proper discrimination will be the result. This discrimination consists in understanding everything in its proper light; in seeing that the *guṇas* have nothing whatever to do with the *puruṡa*, the seer, who is ever free and all bliss. It is only by the force of this junction that the ever-absolved soul *believes* himself bound and miserable, and therefore, the cause of this junction being dissolved by proper knowledge, the soul must necessarily realise himself. The ever-absolved and blissful nature of the soul is called *Kaivalya*—Isolation—a state not limited by any conditions. This is *Mokṡa*, absolution of the last and highest degree.

XXVI. The means of dissolving is continuous discrimination.

Discrimination is already defined above under the preceding aphorism; and it might be added that when true discrimination is arrived at, the senses all bend inward and see nothing but the internal soul, the real essence of all. Discrimination will be of no use if one receives glimpses of it now and then, but it must become a formed and continuous, living, habit, without admitting of intermission even for a twinkling of the eye. This practice of discrimination is the means of dissolving ignorance, the cause of the junction leading to varied experience.

XXVII. The enlightenment which is the last stage, is sevenfold in his case.

In his case, *i. e.*, in the case of one in whom the enlightenment described in XXVI. has taken place. Such enlightenment is indeed the last stage of *Yoga*, for it is the condition of proper *samâdhi* or *vṛttinirodha*. The seven stages are arranged in the order of the proximity of each to the desired end which is the last stage. These are divided into groups of four and three, the first relating to the objective and the second to the subjective. (1) I have known all that was to be known, and nothing further remains to know. (2) I have freed myself from all bonds of every description. (3) By attaining to *Kaivalya*, I have attained everything and nothing more remains. (4) I have done the whole of my duty. (5) My mind is at rest. (6) The *guṇas* have all dropped away, even like stones from the mountain-top, never to rise up again. (7) Being void of the *guṇas* 'I am what I am,' ever free and all bliss. These are the seven stages, which are described in various ways with some slight variation of wording by different commentators. The import, however, is as plain as can be; for each of these stages has the entire cessation of each of the seven states of the mind respectively—*viz.* (1) desire for knowledge; (2) desire for freedom; (3) desire for bliss; (4) desire to do ones duty; (5) sorrow, (6) fear; (7) doubt.

XXVIII. From the practice of the accessories of *Yoga* (arises) enlightenment, by the destruction of impurity, (leading to) discrimination.

This aphorism points out the way to the enlightenment leading to discrimination, by the destruction of impurity, *i. e.*, causes of distraction.

XXIX. Forbearance, observance, posture, regulation of breath, abstraction, contemplation, absorption, trance, are the eight accessories of *yoga*.

These will be explained, and their division into extrinsic and intrinsic will also be shown. The enumeration is made in the order of importance and succession.

XXX. Forbearance consists in abstaining from killing, falsehood, theft, incontinence, and greediness.

Forbearance means such control over mind, body, and speech, as would prevent the student from falling into any of the five errors pointed out. The first and most important of these is killing. It is difficult to give the whole import of the word *himsá* in one word, and I have translated it by killing for want of a better term. It means the wishing evil to any being by word, act, or thought, and abstinence from this kind of killing is the only thing strongly required. It obviously implies abstinence from animal food inasmuch as it is never procurable without direct or indirect *himsâ* of some kind. The avoidance of animal food from another point of view is also strongly to be recommended, as it always leads to the growth of animality to the complete obscuration and even annihilation of intuition and spirituality. It is to secure this condition of being ever with nature and never against it, or in other words being in love with nature, that all other restrictions are prescribed. The next requirement is abstaining from falsehood, that is, from telling what we do not know or believe to be the exact state of things. Theft, the third thing to be avoided, includes, besides actual illegal appropriation, even the thought for any such gain. So also does incontinence, the fourth danger in the path of success, include, besides physical enjoyment, even talking to, looking at, or thinking of the other sex, with lustful intention. The last is greediness which consists not only in coveting more than necessary, but also in keeping in possession anything beyond the very necessaries of life. Several practitioners are known to carry this requirement to the extent of even not accepting anything whatever from others.

XXXI. These, not qualified by class, place, time, or utility, are called great vows, being universal.

Several persons begin the practice of Forbearance, but in a limited sense; as when they resolve that they will not kill the cow or the man, or will abstain from telling lies on certain days and at certain places, or will never do such and such prohibited acts but in pursuance of utility, *i. e.*, when the ends justify the means. All such qualified vows are not good, for those only are really great good vows which are observed universally without any consideration of class, time, place, or utility.

XXXII. Observances consist in purity, contentment, mortification, study, and resignation to *Iśvara*.

The duties hitherto described are negative or of the kind of omission; those enjoined here are positive or of commission. Purity is both bodily and mental, which latter consists in universal love and equanimity. Contentment is the being satisfied with ones lot. The other three are described at the beginning of this section.

XXXIII. The constant pondering upon the opposites (is necessary) when (these) are obstructed by inadequate thoughts.

The *Bhojavṛtti* is not clear on this aphorism. The interpretation is therefore given after the *Bhâṣya* and the *Maṇiprabhâ.* Whenever any or all of the ten duties indicated under *yama* (Forbearance) and *niyama* (Observance) are not fully sustained on account of other inadequate thoughts, the best way to escape from these thoughts is to think upon their opposites. For example, when abstinence from killing is disturbed by a desire to kill, the way to eliminate the disturbing element is by thinking upon its opposite, *viz.*, the quality of love which one who is devoted to *yoga* must possess, and which, if given up, will only lead to endless misery. Similarly for each of the rest. The rule here briefly indicated is of the greatest practical use to beginners.

XXXIV. Inadequate thoughts are killing, &c.; whether done, caused to be done, or approved of; whether arising from covetousness, anger, or delusion; whether slight, middling, or great;—(always) resulting in endless and innumerable misery and ignorance. Hence the (necessity of) pondering upon the opposites.

This aphorism amplifies the reasons for the preceding. Inadequate thoughts are, as already said, killing, &c., meaning the ten opposites of the ten things enjoined. Each of these is shown to be of 27 kinds, by showing its nature, cause, and degree, though it is possible, by multiplying the subdivision, to carry it on *ad infinitum.* And in common practice we daily observe how, in thousand ways and one, each of these evils works its way. The main object of the division is, however, to show that all acts, whether direct or indirect, whether from self-love or mere vengeance, whether appreciable or inappreciable, are all inadequate, and have nothing but endless misery and ignorance as their fruit. Thinking upon these consequences is also a kind of thinking upon the opposite and should be practised. The chief end of such thought ought to be the confirmation of the habit of the opposite of these inadequate thoughts, *viz.*, abstinence from killing, &c.

XXXV. Abstinence from killing being confirmed, there is suspension of antipathy in the presence of him (who has acquired the virtue).

The abstinence here implied is not the merely negative state of not-killing, but the positive feeling of universal love as explained under XXX. When one has acquired this confirmed habit of the mind, even natural antipathy is held in abeyance in his presence; needless to add that no one harms or injures him. All beings, men, animals, birds,—approach him without fear and mix with him without reserve.

XXXVI. Veracity being confirmed, there is the result of the fruits of acts (in him who has acquired the virtue.)

When entire and unswerving truthfulness is fully established, all thoughts and words become immediately effective. What others get by acts such as great sacrifices, &c., he gets by mere thought or word.

XXXVII. Abstinence from theft being confirmed, all jewels approach (him who has acquired the virtue).

When one has given up self-love and thereby the desire for misappropriation, he stumbles at every step on wealth, without actually seeking for it.

XXXVIII. Vigour is obtained on the confirmation of continence.

It is a well-known physiological law that the semen has great connection with the intellect, and we might add the spirituality of men. The abstaining from waste of this important element of being, gives power, the real occult power, such as is desired. No *Yoga* is ever reported successful without the observance of this rule as an essential preliminary.

XXXIX. Abstinence from greediness being confirmed there arises knowledge of the how and wherefore of existence.

When desire is destroyed, when in fact even the last and subtle but unconquerable desire for life too is given up, there arises knowledge of the why and wherefore of existence.

XL. From purity (arises) disgust for one's own body, and non-intercourse with others.

The purity here referred to is physical or external; mental or internal will be dealt with in the following aphorism. One who has understood purity naturally looks with disgust upon his physical body which is full of impurities, and hence feels no strong desire to associate with others.

XLI. Moreover, (there arise) clear passivity, pleasantness of mind, fixity of attention, subjugation of the senses, and fitness for communion with soul.

The results here enumerated are the consequences of mental purity. The meaning is plain enough.

XLII. Superlative happiness (arises) from contentment.

XLIII. (There arise) from mortification, after the destruction of impurities, occult powers in the body and the senses.

It is well-known that the inner sense becomes developed in proportion to the mortification of the flesh; and various methods, more or less severe, are practised in all religions. The occult powers of the body and the senses here referred to consist in what are generally known as second sight, levitation, &c. These, though the beginning and sign of real power (*Yogabala*), are not the true end.

XLIV. By study (is produced) communion with the desired deity.

The constant, silent, and devoted repetition of certain formulæ is said to be efficacious in establishing a sort of mediumistic communication with the higher elementals of nature; as also in developing the inner vision of the student.

XLV. From resignation to *Iśvara* (follows) the accomplishment of *Samâdhi.*

The meaning is sufficiently plain, if we bear in mind the full import of the phrase 'resignation to *Iśvara*.'

XLVI. Posture is that which is steady and easy.

Having described *Yama* and *Niyama*, the first two accessories of *Yoga*, it is proposed to describe the third, *A'sana* or posture. Though numerous variations of the mode of keeping the body in position at the time of performing *Yoga* are given in different books, the general and most convenient definition of posture is that it should be perfectly steady and should cause no painful sensation, never mind what shape it takes. (For further particulars see Appendix.)

XLVII. By mild effort and meditation on the endless.

This aphorism must be read as a part of the preceding. Posture is that which is steady and easy, being so made, by mild effort and meditation on the endless. All violent effort in assuming any particular posture leads to pain and therefore unsteadiness. By slow and mild effort any kind of posture will be acquired as a habit, and it will be easy to assume that posture at a moment's thought, as also to remain in it for a long period of time. After any posture is assumed, it is good to sever our thought entirely from the posture and fix it upon the infinite, say *âkâśa* or *Iśvara* or, as some copies have it, the *Ananta*, meaning, the great serpent that is believed to uphold the earth, &c. These conditions will render the posture entirely painless.

XLVIII. Then no assaults from the pairs of opposites.

The pairs of opposites are heat and cold, pleasure and pain, love and sorrow, &c., constituting the whole of our worldly experience. When one proper posture is fully mastered, effects of the 'pairs of opposites' are not at all felt. It is necessary to obtain such mastery over any one posture before proceeding further.

XLIX. This being (accomplished), *prâṇâyâma* (follows), —the cutting off of the course of inspiration and expiration (of the breath).

Having described the fourth accessory of *Yoga*, it is proposed to describe here the nature of the fifth which is *prâṇâyâma* or control of the breath. It consits of suspending the natural course of the breath, viz., expiration and inspiration.

L. (It is) external, internal, or steady; regulated by place, time, and number; and is long or short.

Prâṇayâma is of four kinds. Three of these are described here, and the fourth is described in the following aphorism. When the breath is expired, or held out as it is technically called, it is *rechaka*, the first *prâṇâyâma*. When it is drawn in, it is the second, called *puraka*. And when it is suspended, all at once, it is the third, called *kumbhaka*. Each of these is regulated by place, time &c. By place is meant the inside or outside of the body, and the particular length* of the breath in the act. Time is the time of the

* Length as given in books on *svara* where the length of the breath is said to vary in accordance with the prevailing *tattva*. It is calculated that the breath is respectively 12,16,4,8, and 0,

duration of each of these, which is generally counted by what is called *mâtrâ*, a measure almost answering to our second; but any convenient measure will serve. When all three kinds of *prâṇâyâma* are combined in one single act, the time varies as 1, 4, 2, for *puraka*, *kumbhaka* and *rechaka*, respectively. Number refers to the number of times the *prâṇâyâma* is done. Works on *Yoga* say that the number should slowly and slowly be carried to so far as eighty, every time one sits for the practice. There are other works which say that the number must be sufficient to enable the student to mark the first *udghâta* and follow it afterwards. *Udghâta* appears to mean the rising of the breath from the navel, and its striking at the roof of the palate. *Prâṇâyâma* has as its chief object the mixing of *prâṇa*, the upper breath, and *apâna* the lower breath, and raising them upwards, by degrees and stages, till they subside in the head. This practice awakens a peculiar force which is dormant about the navel, and is called *Kundalini*. It is this force which is the source of all occult powers. The general practice is to begin with *rechaka* followed by *puraka* by the same nostril, and *kumbhaka* followed by *rechaka* at the opposite nostril, whence the course is begun over again with *puraka* and onward. This is called one *prâṇâyâma*. (For further particulars see Appendix.) It is long or short according to the period for which it is practised.

LI. The fourth is that which has reference to the internal and external subject.

The steady kind of *prâṇâyâma* called *kumbhaka* is a stopping of the inspiration and expiration of the breath without

---

finger-breadths long, according as the *tattva* is *pṛthvi*, *apas*, *tejas*, *vâyu* or *âkâśa*. This, again, externally as well as internally.

reference to its internal or external position. Hence it is remarked under aphorism L., that it is practised only till the first *udghâta* is marked. When this state is reached the *prâṇâyâma* that is practised is the fourth. It considers the position of the breath in the various *padmas**, and carries it, slowly and slowly, stage by stage, to the last *padma* where complete *samâdhi* ensues. Externally it takes into consideration the length of the breath in accordance with the *tattva*, &c. Particular occult powers develop themselves at each stage of progress. The conditions of time, &c., given in aphorism L., are applicable to this also.

LII. Thence is destroyed the covering of light.

By light is here meant the light of entire passivity which is identical with that of the soul, ever blissful and free. The covering consist of the phenomenon which is a result of *karma*. By the practice of *prâṇâyâma* this covering is removed and the real nature of the soul is realised for once, and for ever.

LIII. The mind becomes fit for absorption.

The mind then becomes fit for being quite absorbed in the subject thought of (*i. e.*, *dhâraṇâ*). It is *prâṇâyâma* which leads the way to this stage, before describing which the author

---

* The *padmas* are supposed to be plexuses formed by nerves and ganglia at different places in the body. They are generally believed to be 7 in number, and are called *âdhâra* (at the annus), *adhisthâna* (between the navel and the penis), *maṇipura* (at the navel), *anâhata* (at the heart), *viśuddhi* (in the throat), *âjnâ* (between the eyebrows) and *sahasrâra* (in the pineal gland [?]). A full description of the processes regulating the relation and management of the *prâṇa* in reference to these would require a small volume to itself.

proceeds to describe the immediately next, viz., *pratyâhâra* or abstraction.

LIV. Abstraction is, as it were, the imitating by the senses, the thinking principle, by withdrawing themselves from their objects.

Abstraction consists in the senses becoming entirely assimilated to or controlled by the mind. They must be *drawn away* from their objects and fixed upon the mind, and assimilated to it, so that by preventing the transformations of the thinking principle, the senses also will follow it and be immediately controlled. Not only this but they will be ever ready to contribute collectively towards the absorbing meditation of any given thing at any moment, and even always.

LV. Then follows the greatest mastery over the senses.

The kind of mastery described is hinted at under aphorism LIV. The advantages resulting from this power to a *Yogin* are too plain to require description.

THE YOGA-SUTRA.

SECTION III.

I. Contemplation is the fixing of the mind on something.

Having described the means of purifying the inner self and of avoiding distractions, the author proceeds to point out the proper way to the final end, *Samâdhi*. *Dhâraṇâ* or contemplation is the fixing of the mind on something, external or internal. If internal, it may be one of the plexuses described in the last section, or the tip of the tongue, or the nose, or any convenient spot; if external, it may be any suitable image of the deity, or a picture, or any similar object. Of course it is necessary to bear in mind that any such thing contemplated upon externally or internally should be strictly associated with nothing but holiness and purity. The mind should be able to picture to itself the object even in its absence in all vividness and at an instant's notice.

II. The unity of the mind with it is absorption.

Absorption or *dhyâṇa* is the entire fixing of the mind on the object thought of, to the extent of making it one with it. In fact the mind should, at the time, be conscious only of itself and the object.

III. The same, when conscious only of the object, as if unconscious of itself, is trance.

Absorption carried to the extent of forgetting the act, and of becoming the thing thought of, is trance or *Samâdhi*. It would at once be seen that *Samâdhi* implies two distinct states of consciousness unified in one. The first, which is trance proper, is the forgetting of all idea of the act, and the second, the more important factor, is the becoming the object thought upon. Mere passive trance is a dangerous practice, as it leads to the madness of irresponsible mediumship. It is therefore necessary to lay stress upon the second part of the connotation of the term *Samâdhi*. The three stages, contemplation, absorption, and trance, are, in fact, stages of contemplation, for the thing thought upon, the thinker, and the instrument, together with other things which are attempted to be excluded are all present in the first; all except the last are present in the second, and nothing but the thing is present in the third. Trance, however, is not complete *Yoga*, for it is only *Savikalpa* or conscious-*Samâdhi*, having something to rest upon.

IV. The three together constitute *Samyama*.

Samyama is a technical name for the three inseparable processes taken collectively. When the three are successively practised with respect to one and the same object, at any one time, it is called *Samyama*. *Samyama* is the way to several occult powers, as also to *Nirvikalpa* (or unconscious) *Samâdhi* the *Yoga* proper, as will just be described.

V. By mastering its (results) lucidity of the intellect.

The meaning is sufficiently obvious.

VI. It is used by stages.

It, that is, *Samyama* is to be used by stages. One cannot pass all at once to the highest kind of *Samyama*, any more than one can think of something without first knowing it. It is suggested, for example, that when *Samyama* is practised with respect to, say, a mental image the process will tend from contemplating upon the gross to the subtile. The image may be thought of in all parts; then without the decorations; then without limbs; then without any special identity; and lastly as not apart from "self." The stages here referred to apply generally to a distinction of the kind just shown; but as applied to *Samâdhi* they may mean even the stages shown in aphorisms XXVII. (Section II.) or in XVII. (Section I.).

VII. The three are more intimate than the others.

The other five accessories of *Yoga*, described in section II, are comparatively foreign to the subject of *Yoga* proper. For they are only the preliminaries to *Yoga* which really consists in the three acts described here. Hence these three are more intimate than the others, and are brought out for separate description in a separate section. The first five accessories are called the external means of *Yoga*, for they are useful only in obviating distractions. These three are called internal inasmuch as they are the *Yoga* proper.

VIII. Even it is foreign to the unconscious.

Unconscious or *asamprajnâta-samâdhi* is the final end, or *Yoga*; and looking to that, this *Samyama* also is foreign, as being merely preparatory. In *samyama* there is something to depend upon and hence it is foreign to real *samâdhi* wherein there is nothing to depend upon.

IX. Intercepted transformation is the transformation of the mind into the moment of interception;—

the impressions of distraction and interception going out, and rising up, respectively.

It is very difficult to put this and the following four or five aphorisms into proper English. The point raised for solution is this. It is the nature of the mind which consists of the three *Guṇas*, to keep up transforming itself, without intermission, and when we say that *Samyama* is foreign to unconscious-*Samâdhi*, the question naturally suggests itself, what the mind transforms itself into, in that state? The short, simple answer is that the mind transforms itself into *Nirodha* which I have translated by the word interception, meaning the interception of all transformations, or thought, or distractions. The distractions here implied are not the ordinary distractions described in the preceding sections, but the distraction which is still there, in the form of *Samprajnâta* or concious-*Samâdhi*, the result of *Samyama*. As compared with the highest or unconscious-*Samâdhi*, conscious-*Samâdhi* is a distraction no doubt, for there is yet something which the mind entirely transforms itself into. The moment the mind begins to pass from the one state into the other, two distinct processes begin, *viz.*, the slow but sure going out of the impressions that distract, and the equally gradual but certain rise of the impressions that intercept. When the intercepting impressions gain complete supremacy, the moment of interception is achieved, and the mind transforms itself into this intercepting moment, so to speak. It is in the interval of this change that the mind *may* drop and fall into what is called *laya* or a state of passive dullness leading to all the miseries of irresponsible mediumship. Hence this passage from the conscious to the so-called unconscious is a very difficult and critical process. This *samâdhi* is called *Nirodhapariṇâma* or the transformation of the mind into interceptions. It is called *Dharmaparinâma* or the transformation of the thing's property as will be seen in aphorism XIII.

X. Its flow becomes steady by impressions.

The intercepting impressions must rise so often as to become a habit; for then alone will their flow become deep and steady, and lead to the highest *Samâdhi*. The mind is as it were quite annihilated for no transformation exists. The permanence of this state is all that is desired.

XI. Trance-transformation is the setting and rising of distractions and concentration respectively.

The words *kṡaya* and *udaya* in the original refer to setting and rising, and no more, as will be explained in aph. XIV. The arguments started under aph. IX are here carried further. The explanation here refers to the time when unconscious-*Samadhi* is accomplished. By distractions is here meant that distraction of the mind which draws it off from unconscious-*Samâdhi*, which is the meaning of the word concentration here. Interceptions, being repeated, gain a certain firmness and ripen into unconscious-*Samâdhi*. Hence when this stage is reached the mere negative condition become as it were positive, and there arises concentration on nothing, to use a paradoxical phrase. The moment when the mind arrives at this stage in its transformations is called *lakṡaṇaparinâma* as will be seen in aph. XIII.

XII. Then again the repressed and the revived are equally (present in) consciousness:—this is that

condition of the mind which is transformation into unity.

This aphorism explains the condition of the mind at the moment of complete unconscious-*Samâdhi*. The mind is conscious of nothing except the respective repression and revival (see aph. XIV.) of certain impressions, *viz.*, distractions and interceptions both welded in one act of supreme consciousness. This is called *Avasthâpariṇâma* or transformation as to condition as will be just seen. The mind has its property first transformed. Then this property is joind to a certain moment of time, when the first transformation becomes perfectly ripe and indicates the real condition of the mind. Then it is easy to see that transformation though essentially one is, for the sake of explanation and analysis, described as threefold.

XIII. By this the three, property-, character-, and condition-transformations are explained.

The theory of the transformation of the mind is extended to all objects, for there is nothing which is not compounded of one or more or all of the three *guṇas* which are ever in a state of transformation. When the very property of a thing is altered it is called property-transformation or *dharmapariṇâma*. When afterwards the thing with its altered property becomes manifest in relation to some time, past, present, or future, it is called its (rather its property's) character-transformation or *lakśaṇapariṇâma*, for without the limitation of time it is difficult to characterise or define the nature of any conceivable entity. When after this the particular property thus defined ripens into maturity or decay, it is called its condition-transformation or *avasthâpariṇâma*. Thus the whole universe consists of nothing but certain objects, and their properties which latter by their transformations produce all variety. Thus this philosophy puts forth an explanation of the phenomenal universe, in consonance with the doctrines of the *Sânkhya*; and *Vijnânabhikśu* remarks that the *Vedânta*-theory of *Mâyâ* is not quite discordant to this. It remains to explain what the object or the substratum—*dharmi*—is, and to this we now proceed.

XIV. The substratum is that which is correlated to properties, tranquil, active, or indescribable.

The doctrine *Ex nihilo nihil fit* is carried out to its full extent by this school and therefore it is held that anything can never manifest itself in any other thing unless it previously existed there. This manifestation has reference only to the properties of things, and it cannot be said what will come out of what. In fact everything is producible from everything for every thing potentially exists in the root of all, *i.e., prakṛti*. All this, however, takes place in relation to the *form* in which a thing manifests itself, and this form is none other than the unique combination of the three original properties. The properties can never exist but in relation to some subsratum which, in its turn, can never become cognisable but through the properties. The properties which have once manifested themselves and passed into oblivion are called tranquil, for they have played their part and are still there to become actively manifest some other day. Those that are seen at any moment are called active; whereas others not yet manifest are consigned to the realm or possibility of the indescribable. In other words, these possible manifestations are as yet latent. After this explanation it is easy to see that the object or the substratum (of properties) is that which is correlated to the properties in one or other of the three states.

XV. The cause in the mutability of forms is the change of order.

From the preceding explanation it is clear that whatever form anything mainfests itself as the phenomena is nothing more than a mere succession of properties in one or other of the conditions described in aph. XIII. The universe with all its phenomena is nothing more than an incessant and immediate succession of states of properties. This need not imply the *Buddhist* or rather *Mâdhyamika* doctrine of *Kṡaṇás* or moments, which looks upon everything as made of nothing but an unbroken series of moments presented to consciousness; for here it is the properties alone which follow one upon the other in succession, the thing itself remaining unaltered.

XVI. The knowledge of past and future, by *Samyama* on the three transformations.

The transformations are those described in aph. XIII. By performing *Samyama* on them, the past and future of their substratum is at once revealed to the mind.

XVII. The word, its sense, and knowledge, are confused with one another on account of their being mutually mistaken for one another; hence by *Samyama* on the proper province of each, (arises) the comprehension of (the meaning of) sounds uttered by any being.

Every school of philosophy has its own theory about the relation between word and meaning, but it would be sufficient here to observe that the *Yoga*-philosophy accepts what is generally known as the *Sphota*-doctrine. *Sphota* is a something indescribable which eternally exists apart from the letters forming any word, and is yet inseparably connected with it, for it *reveals** itself on the utterance of that word. In like manner the meaning of a sentence is also *revealed*, so to speak, from the collective sense of the words used. So then, the eternal sense of a word is always different from the letters making that word; and the knowledge which, in its turn, is conveyed to our mind is also equally apart from these two. The sense of words is generally classified under four heads: objects, properties, actions, and abstractions; and the impression into which our mind transforms itself at the moment of cognising is the knowledge produced. In ordinary intercourse it so happens that the letters, the sense, and the knowledge, all are so confused together as not to be separable from one another. Thus letters, *i. e.*, sounds being confused with the sense and knowledge, convey no precise meaning if they happen to be beyond our previous acquaintance. The fact, however, is that every meaning is eternally existent, and is as eternally connected with particular sounds,† and therefore conveys or *reveals* the same sense wherever it is uttered. Therefore by performing *Samyama* on the three separately, the *Yogin* can comprehend the sense of all sounds uttered by any sentient being in nature. Even so can the music of nature be heard; and the joyous *nâda* within be cognised and understood.

---

* Whence the name *Sphota* (that which is revealed).

† For letters are but the vehicles of the different sounds arising from the 8 places within the body, *viz.*, the chest, the larynx, the root of the tongue, the teeth, the lips, the palate, the nose, and the head. Hence the divisions, &c., of letters.

XVIII. By mental presentation of the impressions, a knowledge of former class.

By performing *Samyama* which is the same thing as complete mental presentation as described in the aphorism, on the impressions inhering in the mind from time immemorial, there arises knowledge of the class, &c., to which one belongd in previous incarnations. These impressions are of two kinds, the first producing simply a memory of previous experiences, and the second leading to the conditions described in aph. XIII. Sec. II. As therefore the conditions of any being at any moment are only a result of these latent impressions fulfilling themselves, it is possible to understand their connection with the past by *Samyama*, as described.

XIX. With reference to a sign, the knowledge of the mind of others.

When the *Yogin* performs *Samyama* with reference to any sign such as the complexion, the voice, or any such thing, he at once understands the state of the mind of which these are the sure indices. Any body's mind can thus be easily comprehended by the *Yogin*.

XX. But not with its occupant, for that is not the subject.

It is said in the preceding aphorism that the state of the mind of any being can be understood. It is now asserted that the state of the mind may be understood, but not the thought which occupies it, for there is no sign belonging to the object of that thought brought directly under *Samyama*. If, however, after ascertaining the state of the mind, the *Yogin* performs *Samyama* on the subject occupying it, he will comprehend that also.

XXI. By *Samyama* on the form of the body, the power of comprehension being suspended, and the connection between light and the eye being severed, there follows disappearance of the body.

The theory is that when light, the property of *sattva*, emanates from our body and becomes united with the organ of sight which again is a reservoir of similar light, visual perception follows. When, therefore, the *Yogin* performs *Samyama* on the form of his body, *i. e.*, the property that endows visibility to his body, he disserves the connection between the light from his body and the eye of the cogniser, and thus follows the disappearance of his body. The *Yogin* in fact centres all visibility in his thinking principle and prevents the perception of his body. The same holds true of the other organs of sense, and hence of sounds, sensations, &c.*

XXII. *Karma* is of two kinds: active and dormant; by *Samyama* on them (results) knowledge of cessation; as also by portents.

That *karma* which produces its results speedily and is actually on the way to bear fruit is called active; whereas that which is only in a latent condition of potency is called dormant. By performing *Samyama* on these two classes of *karma*, the *Yogin* knows the time of the cessation of his life,

---

* Some copies make this part of the commentary a separate aphorism by itself.

i. e., death. He knows at once which *Karma* will produce what fruit and therefore at once sees the conditions of his death.

The same knowledge arises also from portents, in the case of a *Yogin*. Portents are corporeal, celestial, or physical. The corporeal are such as the inaudibility of the *prâṇa* in the stomach on closing the ears. The celestial are such as the sight of things generally regarded invisible, as heaven, &c. The physical consist in seeing extraordinary or frightful beings, &c. These and similar portents, such as dreams, the chance hearing of particular words, &c., indicate, to use a common expression, which way the wind blows. But none but *Yogins* can make any use of such portents, for it is only they who can precisely interpret them.

XXIII. In sympathy, &c., strength.

By performing *samyama* with reference to sympathy, &c., as described in aph. XXXIII, Sect. I., each of the feeling becomes so strong as to produce the desired result at any moment. Sympathy, compassion, and complacency, are the three things referred to here, for indifference does not require to be made an object of *Samyama*. Whoever has performed the *Samyama* here described finds no difficulty in enlisting the good will and friendship of any one at any moment.

XXIV. In strength, that of the elephant, &c.

By performing *Samyama* on the powers of any animal, the *Yogin* acquires those powers.

XXV. The knowledge of the subtile, the obscure, and the remote, by contemplation on the inner light.

The inner light here referred to is already explained in aph. XXXVI, Sect. I. It is the light of the quality of *sattva* which is clear and all-penetrating. When this is seen by the *Yogin*, he may continue to contemplate, *i. e.*, perform *Samyama* upon this light with reference to anything he wants to know, and in his internal consciousness will be intuitively revealed the knowledge of subtile things such as the invisible atoms, obscure things such as hidden treasures and mines, and things which are very inapproachably remote.

XXVI. By *Samyama* on the sun, the knowledge of space.

By space is here meant the space intercepted between the sun and the earth.

XXVII. In the moon, the knowledge of the starry regions.

The commentaries say that *Samyama* on the moon is necessary for a knowledge of the starry regions, for the stars are obscured in the light of the sun.

XXVIII. In the pole-star, knowledge of their motions.

By *Samyama* on the pole-star is produced knowledge of the relative motions and positions of stars and planets.

XXIX. In the navel-circle, the knowledge of the arrangement of the body.

The *chakras*, circles, or plexuses, have been described before, under the name of *padma*. The most important of these, so far as the arrangement of the nerves of the body is concerned, is the *nâbhi-chakra* called *maṇipura*. It is the pivot of the whole system. Hence *Samyama* on it leads to a knowledge of the conditions of the body. From this aphorism the author begins to describe the *siddhis* connected with the internal body, having finished those connected with the external world.

XXX. In the pit of the throat, the cessation of hunger and thirst.

The pit of the throat is the region about the pharynx where the breath from the mouth and the nostrils meets. It is said that contact of *prâṇa* with this region produces hunger and thirst, which, therefore, may be checked by performing *samyama* on this part to neutralise the effects of the contact. It may be remarked that the fifth *chakra* called *viśuddhi* is situated somewhere about the same region, and any one who is able to concentrate his breath in that *chakra* and upward easily acquires freedom from hunger and thirst, besides other occult powers.

XXXI. In the *Kurma-nâdi*, steadiness.

Kurma-nâdi is the nerve wherein the breath called *kurma** resides ; and *samyama* on this leads to such a fixity of the body as to make it completely steady and immovable.

XXXII. In the light in the head, the sight of the *siddhas*.

The light in the head is explained to be that collective flow of the light of *sattva* which is seen at the *Brahmarandhra*

* Just as the same breath is called *prâṇa*, &c., according to the place where it works, so the same is called *Nâga*, *Kurma*, *Kṛkala*, *Devadatta* and *Dhananjaya* according to the functions it performs.

which is variously supposed to be somewhere near the coronal artery, the pineal gland, or over the medula oblongata. Just as the light of a lamp burning within the four walls of a house presents a luminous appearance at the key-hole, so even does the light of *sattva* show itself at the crown of the head. This light is very familiar to all acquainted even slightly with *Yoga*-practices and is seen even by concentration on the space between the eyebrows. By *Samayama* on this light the class of beings called *siddhas*–popularly known in theosophic circles as *Mahâtmas* or high adepts–able to walk through space unseen, are immediately brought to view, notwithstanding obstacles of space and time.

XXXIII. Or everything from the result of *pratibhâ*.

Pratibhâ is that degree of intellect which developes itself without any special cause, and which is capable of leading to real knowledge. It corresponds to what is generally called intuition. If the *Yogin* tries simply to develope this faculty in himself by performing *samyama* on the intellect he becomes able to accomplish all that is said before, only through the help of *pratibhâ*. This sort of *pratibhâ* is called *târaka-jnâna*, the knowledge that saves, *i.e.*, leads to final absolution—*mokśa*. Hence that *yoga* which entirely concerns itself with this department of intellectual and spiritual development is often called *Târaka-yoga* or *Râjayoga*. It does not appear correct to interpret this *pratibhâ* to mean the star lucifer in accordance with a doubtful expression of the *Bhâśya* (*viz.*, *prâtibham nâma târakam*) after its explanation by *Vâchaspatimiśra* which agrees with the above. In the cultivation of intuition consists the real *power* of *yoga*.

XXXIV. In the heart, knowledge of mind.

By the heart is meant the *chakra* called *anâhata;* and *samyama* on this leads to knowledge of the mind, *viz.*, the mind of others as well as ones own.

XXXV. Experience is the *Indistinctness of the mild* conception of *sattva* and *puruśa* which are absolutely apart; this enjoyment being for another, knowledge of *puruśa* arises from *samyama* on himself.

It has often been remarked in the course of this book that *sattva*, the source of intelligence, is apart and distinct from *puruśa*, the ultimate essence of consciousness. The theory is that *puruśa* being reflected in clear *sattva*, enlivens it; and all experience is assumed by the *sattva* so enlivened to be entirely of its own act. This confused identification of the two, ever distinct by nature, is the cause of all varied experiences. It is plain that the experience which the *sattva* receives is of no use to itself, it is all for the *puruśa*; for all the action of *prakṛti*, the source of *sattva* and the inseparable correlative of *puruśa*, is for *puruśa*. Hence the action of *sattva* is for another, and not for itself. Its *real* function and purpose is to merge itself in the *puruśa*. It is therefore laid down that *samyama* on himself, that is, on his own right nature and purpose, will lead to a clear knowledge of *puruśa*.

XXXVI. Thence is produced intuitional (cognition of) sound, touch, sight, taste, and smell.

The five sensations which constitute the whole of our sense-knowledge, are cognised, after the knowledge described in the preceding aphorism, is produced, simply by intuition *i. e.*, by what is called *pratibhâ* or *târaka-janana*, independently of the conditions of time and space. The reason for this is sought in the fact of *pratibhâ* being at once produced with all its results, as described in aph. XXXIII., on clear knowledge of *puruśa*.

XXXVII. These are obstacles in the way of *Samâdhi*; and are powers in moments of suspension.

These occult powers described hitherto, and to be described hereafter, are positive obstacles in the way of *samâdhi, i.e.*, *Yoga* proper whose nature and import is explained in Sect. I. They serve as obstacles because they become the cause of distracting the mind by the various feelings they excite. But they are not quite useless inasmuch as they are great powers for good in moments when *samâdhi* is suspended.

XXXVIII. The mind enters another body, by relaxation of the cause of bondage, and by knowledge of the method of passing.

The bondage is the *mind's* being bound to a particular body. The cause of limiting the otherwise all-pervading mind to a particular spot is *karma* or *dharma* and *adharma*, *i. e.*, good or bad deeds. When by constant *samyama* on these, the effect of the cause is neutralised and the bonds of confinement loosened, then the mind is free to enter any dead or living organism and perform its functions through it. But for this purpose a knowledge of effecting this transfer is equally necessary. By *samyama* on the nerves which are all constantly pervaded by the mind, the knowledge of the *Chittavahânâdi*, the peculiar nerve which is the passage of the mind, is revealed.

XXXIX. By mastery over *udâna*, ascension, and non-contact with water, mud, thorns, &c.

The physical functions of the vital air pervading the whole body are known by different names as already hinted at in the first note to aph. XXXI. The air intercepted between the tip of the nose and the heart is called *prâna*, that between the heart and the navel is called *samâna*, that from the navel to the fingers of the feet is called *apâna*, that above the tip of the nose is called *udâna*, and that which pervades the whole body is called *vyâna*. The respective functions are—vitalizing, digestion, repulsion of excrements, raising up the sound, &c., and motion in general. The *udâna* has tendency to raise the body upwards and carry it above water, thorns, &c. Hence the necessity of *samyama* on the *udâna*. It is observed that this *samyama* also enables the *Yogin* to die at will.

XL. Effulgence by mastery over *Samâna*.

About the navel is the seat of the *samâna* where it performs the function of digestion by keeping up the internal fire. When *samyama* is performed on the *samâna*, this fire can be seen about the whole body, which will on that account appear effulgent. It is observed that this effulgence is most perceptible about the head, between the eyebrows, and at the navel. It is said to be the basis of the magnetic aura of living beings.

XLI. By *Samyama* on the relation between *âkâśa* and the sense of hearing, (arises) supernatural audition.

Akâśa (ether) is all-pervading, and is the cause of sound, it being its special property. If *samyama* be peformed on *akâśa*, sound of whatever description, at any distance, will be easily heard by the ear.

XLII. By *Samyama* on the relation between the body and *âkâśa*, as also by being identified with light

(things like) cotton, (there follows) passage through space.

It is the *âkâśa* which is all-pervading and keeps things in position; and *samyama* performed on the relation of *âkâśa* with the objects (the body in the present instance) posited therein, will give the object thought of such lightness as to enable it to soar through space, or pass with the rays of the sun, or on water or the mere string of a spider's web. This result follows on account of the resistance of *âkâśa* being subdued, and its all-pervading property being utilized. The same result will follow by performing *samyama* on light things like cotton and thereby rendering the body light to float freely in the air.

XLIII. The external, unthought-of, transformation (of the mind) is the great incorporeal; hence the destruction of the covering of illumination.

The great incorporeal is in *Sanskṛta* called the *Mahâvideha*. The meaning is briefly this. We always think in relation to the ego within us, and therefore in relation to the body. Even when we direct our mind somewhere out of the body, it is still in relation with the thinking self. When this relation is entirely severed and the mind exists as it were spontaneouly, outside and independent of the body, the power that arises is called *Mahâvideha*. In this condition knowledge of any and every description is within easy reach of the ascetic, for it then comes to him without effort, the covering of the three qualities which hinders intuitive *sâttvika* illumination, being broken. It is this state of the internal mind that is most favourable to the *Yogins* passing from one corporeal shape into another, for it is nothing more than the *vṛtti* severed from the body that travels from one place to another. Those familiar with the so-called spirit-materializations will readily comprehend the somewhat obscure sense of this aphorism.

XLIV. Mastery over the elements, by *Samyama* on the gross, the constant, the subtile, the all-pervading, and the fruition-bearing (in them.)

Let it be remarked at the beginning that all the five elements are each to be found in all the five conditions mentioned. In other word, each and every element is made of these five states and no more. A substance or element is not a something that is the substratum of quality or action, as the *Nyâya* and *Vaiśeṣika* will have it ; but it is merely an aggregate of certain generic and specific properties. Every element has first its gross phenomenal form ; then its constant invariable form, as heat in the case of *Tejas*, viscidity in the case of *Jala*, &c.; then its subtile form consisting of the *tanmâtras* or subtle properties ; fourthly its all-pervading form as made up of one or more of the three qualities—*Sattva*, *Rajas*, *Tamas*—which are everywhere ; and lastly, its fruition-bearing form or the form endowed to it for the end which it serves. Thus by performing *samyama* on all these forms, in fact all that makes up the element, the *yogin* acquires mastery over all elements and becomes able to effect anything by the mere force of his will.

XLV. Then the attainment of *aṇimâ* and others, as also of perfection of the body and the corresponding non-obstruction of its functions.

Aṇimâ and others are the eight *siddhis*or high occtult powers. They are *aṇimâ* (the power to assimilate oneself with an atom,) *mahimâ* (the power to expand oneself into space), *laghımâ* (the power to be as light as cotton or any similar thing), *garimâ* (the power to grow as heavy as any thing), *prâpti* (the power of reaching anywhere, even to the moon), *pràkâmya* (the power of having all wishes of whatever description realsied), *iśatva* (the power to create), *vaśitva* (the power to command all). By carrying the *samyama* described in the preceding aphorism to perfection, these powers become manifest in the *Yogin.* Some say that the first five are developed by *samyama* on the gross part of the elements, the sixth by *samyama* on the constant form of the elements, and the rest by *samyama* on the causes of the elements. The next development is in the body of the *Yogin* which is described in the following aphorism; and the corresponding non-obstruction of its functions means the power whereby the form of the body, or its motion, &c., are not affected or obstructed by the effects or barriers of earth, water, fire, &c.

XLVI. Beauty, gracefulness, strength, adamantine-hardness, constitute perfection of the body.

XLVII. Mastery over the organs of sense by *samyama* on the power of cognition, nature, egoism, all-pervasiveness, and fruition-giving capacity (of them).

The five divisions of the constituents of the organs of sense make up the whole of each and every sense and should be understood in the same manner as the five forms alluded to under aph. XLIV., in reference to the elements. The power of cognition refers to the general nature of the senses to cognise; their nature refers to the knowledge which each produces about the subject of cognition ; egoism refers to the individual consciousness that is always present in all acts of *sensing* so to speak; the other two are already explained. By mastering these five things in respect to each and every organ of sense there arises complete mastery over them, the further result whereof is described in the following.

XLVIII. Thence fleetness (as of) mind, the being unobstructed by instruments, and complete mastery over the *pradhâna*.

The powers acquired from complete control over the organs of sense are described in this aphorism. The first consits in such fleetness of the body as is possible only to the mind; the second in the uninterrupted exercise of the senses without the co-ordinate help of the body ; and the third in such mastery over the *pradhâna*—the root of all—as will enable the *Yogin* to command or create anything at will. The *siddhis* or powers described from aph. XLIV. to XLVIII., are called *madhupratikâ*, as sweet as honey, for each of them is as sweet as all of them, like any part or the whole of a comb of honey. Or the word *madhu* may be taken to imply the *ṛtambharaprajnâ*, intuitive cognition ; and that wherein is realised the cause of this intuitive cognition may be called *madhupratikâ*.

XLIX. In him who is fixed upon the distinctive relation of *sattva* and *puruśa*, (arise) mastery over all things and the knowledge of all.

When the *yogin* frees himself from all other things and rests in pure *sattva* and the *puruśa* reflected in it, he acquires the powers named in the aphorism. This *siddhi* is called *Viśokâ* or 'void of all sorrows,' inasmuch as the *Yogin* is henceforward free from all distractions and all obstructions.

L. By non-attachment even thereto, follows *Kaivalya*, the seeds of bondage being destroyed.

When the *yogin* does not attach himself to these occult powers, there is repeated in him the constant impression of non-attachment *(vairâgyasanskâraseśa)*, which leads to the highest end—*kaivalya*, the state of oneness, being one and alone, *viz*., the *puruśa*. This arises on account of all the causes of bondage beginning with *avidyâ*, &c., as described in Sectoin II, being completely and finally destroyed.

LI. (There should be) entire destruction of pleasure or pride in the invitations by the powers (of various places), for there is possibility of a repetition of evil.

Yogins are of four degrees. (1) *Prathamkalpika* or one in the preliminary stage, (2) *Madhupratika* or one who has reached the state of *ṛtambharaprajnâ* or the power called *madhupratikâ*, (3) *Bhutendriyajayi*, one who has obtained mastery over the elements and the senses, in fact over every thing, and (4) *Atikrântabhâvaniya*, one who has attained *kaivalya*. When the *Yogin* passes from the first state and enters the second, his danger begins. He is *en rapport* with those regions that are not amenable to ordinary vision, and is therefore open to danger from the beings of that realm, good, bad, and indifferent. These are called *Devas*—powers of places, *i. e*., powers presiding over various places or forces, such as residence in heaven, company of beautiful women, possession of various elixirs, various events, &c. But besides mere temptations, either seen or unseen, there may be various other ways, both physical as well as spiritual, in which the aspirant may be worried, frightened, or anyhow thrown off his guard, and tempted or ruined. The only remedy for all this mischief is supreme non-attachment which consists in not taking pleasure in the enjoyment of the temptations, as well as in not taking pride in ones power to call up such. A steady calm will carry the *Yogin* safe to the end. If this cannot be done, the very evils from which the *Yogin* seeks release would harass him with redoubled strength.

LII. Discriminative knowledge from *Samyama* on moments and their order.

Kṡaṇa or moment is that infinitesimal portion of time which cannot be further divided. By full contemplation of the moments which make up time and the order in which they follow one another, arises that knowledge which enables the *Yogin* to discriminate everything, for there is nothing which is not related to time.

LIII. From it knowledge of similars, there being non-discrimination by class, characteristic, or position.

Things are destinguished from one another by the class to which they belong; or where they are of the same class by the peculiar characteristics which they possess; or, when they are of the same class and characteristic, by the position they occupy in time or space. But where all these fail and there is no possibility of separating one thing from another, as in a collection of atoms, it is the discriminative knowledge described in the preceding aphorism that helps the *Yogin*.

LIV. The knowledge born of discrimination is *târaka*, relating to all objects, in every condition, and simultaneous.

In aphorism XXXIII. of this section we have already described the nature of *târaka-jnâna*—the knowledge that saves from the bonds of the world. The discriminative knowledge described in aphorism LII. results into *târaka*, the knowledge which is the end and aim of *yoga*. It relates to all objects from the *pradhâna* to the *bhutas*, as also to all conditions of these objects. Moreover it produces knowledge of all things simultaneously and is quite independent of the ordinary rules of cognition. Hence it is the highest knowledge which can be desired by the *yogin*, and it is a sure index of *Kaivalya* to be described in the following aphorism as its result.

LV. *Kaivalya* on the equality of purity between *puruśa* and *sattva*.

We know that *puruśa* is all light, bliss, and ever free; and also that *sattva* the cause of all knowledge and enlightenment is the source of *buddhi* and *ahankâra*. When *sattva*, *i. e.*, the *antahkaraṇa*, becomes so far pacified as to lose all consciousness of action on its own part, then indeed is its purity said to be equal to that of the *puruśa*. Thus when *sattva* is, as it were, annihilated to all purposes, there remains the *puruśa* ever free and all bliss. This state is the state of *kaivalya*, the full import of which word will form the subject of the following Section.

THE YOGA-SUTRA.

SECTION IV.

I. The *Siddhis* are the result of birth, herbs incantations, austerities, or *Samâdhi*.

The object of this Section is to give certain explanations with a view to make clear the nature of *Kaivalya*, the final absolution aimed at by the *Yogin*. It begins with explaining how the *Siddhis* or occult powers are acquired. They are not, as a matter of fact, acquired in one life and hence they may be the result of the accumulated effects of several existences. This indirectly explains how any and every effort in the direction of *Yoga* is never attempted in vain. The powers may be incidental to birth, as the power of flying in birds, or they may be produced by certain herbs and medicines, as the power of living for eternity conferred by certain elixirs. They may be the result of certain incantations or austerities, or above all of the practice, of *Samâdhi* as described in the previous pages.

II. The transformation into another kind (is) by the flow of *Prakṛti*.

The question is this. How is one body changed into another of a different class even in the same existence? It is replied that the flow of *prakṛti* does it all. By the flow of *prakṛti* is meant that inscrutable action of matter which performs all the work of transformation as seen in material beings. The very potencies (*Sanskâra*) of matter do all, and by powerful application produce the necessary conditions for their independent action.

III. The incidental cause is not the real cause in the action of *Prakṛti*; from thence is the removal of obstacles, like a husbandman.

The incidental causes in the production of material results are our virtuous and vicious actions (*Dharmâdharma*). It may be asked if *prakṛti* does all by its action and produces transformations equal to its previous *sanskâras*, where is the use of individual good or bad actions? The performance of such acts is not at all useful in setting up the action of *prakṛti*; but it only prepares the way for its free action by removing, if good, the obstruction in its way. An illustration in point is that of the husbandman who only removes the obstacles in the way of the water which then passes of itself from one spot to another.

IV. Created minds proceed from the sense of being alone.

The question at issue follows directly from the foregoing considerations. If performance of good acts removes all obstacles and prepares the way for the free action of *prakṛti*, a *Yogin* whose vision reveals to him all he has still to go through may wish, as it were, to multiply himself and thus undergo at one and the same time the fruition of all that is to happen. In this case he will require as many minds as there are bodies; and the question is whence do these come, it being taken for granted that a *Yogin* can duplicate his gross body. Such a *Yogin* has full command over *Mahattattva*, the root of all egoism and everything else which makes up 'mind.' The sense of being or individuality is the result of *Mahat*, and the *Yogin* who has command over it is able to send forth as many minds as he likes from this grand reservoir.

V. One mind is the cause of all the minds in their various activities.

This aphorism is put in to explain how the identity of one and the same individual is preserved in all the different bodies with different minds.

VI. That which is born of contemplation is free from impressions.

The minds referred to in aphorism IV. may be of five kinds according to the means resorted to after aphorism I. If the individual with so many duplicates of itself were to acquire new impressions, the purpose of creating these minds will be frustrated, for instead of exhausting all previous impressions by simultaneous fruition new ones will be accumulated. Hence it is pointed out that that which is produced by the fifth kind of means *(samâdhi)* is free from accumulating impressions.

VII. Actions are neither white nor black in the case of *Yogins*; they are of three kinds, in the case of others.

Actions are white, black, mixed, and indifferent. The first are of gods, the second of wicked beings. The third of men and the fourth of *Yogins*. In other words, *Yogins* acquire no impressions by their acts, for they are perfect in non-attachment and hence are ever free. This aphorism is only a corollary of the preceding and explains the meaning with greater clearness.

VIII. From thence, there is development of those impressions alone for which the conditions are favourable.

From thence, meaning, from the three kinds of *Karma*. Every act leaves an impression; and these are collected one upon the other, and new ones added to them, as any of them spends itself away by producing its proper result under proper conditions. The point of the aphorism is to explain how and in what order the various impressions manifest themselves. It says that only those manifest themselves, conditions for which are favourable. For example, if a being who is a man becomes a man again, after passing through the dog, the wolf and the ape, it is certain that such impressions alone will manifest themselves in each and any of these existences as are favoured by the conditions. The impressions for which the conditions are not favourable will lie dormant till their time.

IX. There is the relation of cause and effect even (among them) though separated by class, space, time, on account of the unity of memory and impressions.

The preceding considerations at once suggest a doubt as to the continuity of the various *vâsanâs* or impressions as cause and effect. It is asserted that though *vâsanâs* of a particular kind be interrupted for ages by circumstances of class, time and space not permitting their manifestation, still they are sure to manifest themselves when the proper conditions are secured. To take an example, if one with human *vâsanâs* passes through a series of incarnations other than human, and that too for an inconceivable length of time, still the human *vâsanâs* which were dormant so long will manifest themselves when and where the human conditions are again fulfilled. It may still be argued how this can be? It is answered, by the unity of impressions and memory. Every act leaves some impression which produces memory. Memory in its turn leads to action and fresh impressions. If a child is led by instinct, for example, to act in a particular way, that instinct is proof of a memory which must be the result of its corresponding and inseparable impression left by some act in a previous incarnation, never mind when and where.

X. Besides they are without beginning, on account of the eternity of desire.

They, *i. e.*, the *vâsanâs*. This aphorism solves a difficulty. If the continuity of *vâsanâ* be admitted, previous incarnation must of necessity be regarded as a fact. And if previous incarnation is a fact, there must be a point where actual experience began, and produced the *vâsanâs*. The fact, however, is that *vâsanâ* has no beginning and no end, just like the universe which has no beginning and no end. *Vâsanâ* is concomittant with *desire* or *chitta*, *i. e.*, the mind, generally speaking. Every being has the spontaneous wish 'to be,' and it is this instinctive function of the mind which makes *vâsanâ* inseparable from mind. The mind again is not atomic as the *Naiyâyikas* hold, but all-pervading like *Akâśa* (ether).* Hence *vâsanâ* is everywhere and manifests itself in acts, through memory, wherever the necessary conditions are fulfilled. In fact if there is no *vâsanâ* or desire there is no

* Hence the theory that the *âkâśa* retains attenuated impressions of all our acts, mental or physical, which can at any time be called to life. *A'kâśa* is, therefore, not merely ether, a form of *dead* matter, but something more than that.

world; *vâsanâ* is as it were a law of nature, the very reason of being, and as such has no beginning like all other laws of its kind.

XI. Being held together by cause, effect, substratum, and support, it is destroyed by their destruction.

If *vâsanâ* is eternal, how could it be destroyed? It is replied that it is not eternal in the same sense in which the soul (*Puruśa*) is eternal; but only its current is eternal. Hence on the destruction of the cause or causes which set it a-going it is possible to destroy it too. *Avidyâ* or ignorance is the cause which produces egoism, which in its turn leads to good or bad actions. These produce the results which leave certain impressions. Thus the circle of *vâsanâ* never ends. The cause which produces *vâsanâ* is action, the effects being class, age, and fruition. The substratum is the thinking principle, the supports being the various objects cognised. When proper *Yoga*-training and knowledge dertroy these causes, their results, *viz*., *vâsanâs*, are at once annihilated and *Kaivalya* follows.

XII. Past and future exists in real nature, in consequence of the difference in the conditions of the properties.

The question is, how can *vâsanâs* which do exist somehow be entirely annihilated? The indestructibility of matter would not admit the assumption of such a position. The explanation is sought for in the peculiar theory of this philosophy which regards everything as having in it, by way of potentiality (called *śakti*), the seeds of all its *forms* or *vâsanâs*, past, present and future.* The mind experiences these according as they become ripe for fruition; but the distinction laid down is that fruition consists in nothing more than the manifestation of future properties. One who has got proper illumination reduces even the future, besides the present, to the past, and herein is contained the real import of the oft-told doctrine that all acts of the enlightened are like the sowing of seeds baked on fire. Hence when all *vâsanâs* are reduced to the past, the mind is said to be entirely free—in eternal *Kaivalya*—its own as well as the *vâsanâs'* existence notwithstanding.

XIII. They are manifest or subtile being of the nature of the *Guṇas*.

It is just said that the past and the future exisit, in its real nature. What this nature is, is shown in this aphorism. They meaning the conditions of the properties are either manifest, that is experienced in the present; or subtile, that is yet to come. They are all, from *Mahat* down to any individual object, of the nature of the *Guṇas*. That is to say they are mere transformations of the three *Guṇas* and are nothing apart from them. Every object in whatever condition is pleasant, painful, or indifferent, and this is nothing but the result of its primal constitution. The *Guṇas* keep up transforming themselves every minute, and produce the panorama of various phenomena. It is well said "the *form* of the *Guṇas* is never visible, that which is so is but false show, entirely worthless."

* Hence it is laid down in *Sutra XVI.*, Section III, that *Samyama* on the three *pariṇâmas* produces knowledge of the past, present and the future.

XIV. In consequence of the unity of transformation (results) the one-ness of things.

The question naturally arises, how any given thing which is a mere transformation of the three *Guṇas* is cognised as a unique fact of mental perception, if each of the three *Guṇas*, which enter into its formation, have their peculiar transformations? The answer is that the *Guṇas* do not act independently of one another, any one of them necessarily subordinates the other two. The transformation, then, becomes perfectly coherent and is capable of being presented as one unique object. This can be easily seen even in the categories of the *Sânkhya*. For example, *Mahat*, which is one individual substance, so to speak, is nothing more than a transformation of the three *Guṇas* in which *Sattva* is subordinate. From *Mahat* arise *Ahankâra*, and the five *Tanmatrâs* according as *Rajas* or *Tamas* is predominant. All the same, each of these transformations is always known as one.

XV. Though things are similar, the cause of mind and things is distinct in consequence of the difference of minds.

The preceding considerations establish, in an indirect manner, the existence of things as objects external to the mind. The *Vijnânavâdi-Bauddhas* who maintain that things are but the reflections of our thinking principle, would object to such a position. The objection could not bear examination; for the existence of things apart from the thinking principle is certain. Though there is, indeed, complete similarity among objects of the same class, still the way in which the objects affect the mind, and the way in which the mind is affected by them, are entirely distinct. Hence objects exist out of the thinking principle. Though objects are similar they are not presented to different minds in the same light, which shows that they are apart from the mind. Again we often hear more than one person saying that he has seen the same object as is seen by another. This would prove that though the object is one, the cognisers are many. This circumstance proves the distinction of the object and the mind. Again the seer and the sight, *i. e.*, the mind and the object, or the instrument of knowledge and the object of knowledge, cannot be one and the same, for then all distinctive knowledge will be impossible, which, however, is absurd. To attempt a solution of this difficulty by saying that eternal *vâsanâ* of the form of external objects is the cause of all our distinctive knowledge is useless, for that which has already spent itself cannot become the cause. Hence objective existence must be granted as independent of the subject. Nor should it be imagined how one substance (*viz.*, *Prakṛti*) could produce in this case all the multifarious differences of our experience, for the three *Guṇas* and their various combinations in different degrees are enough to account for all that. In the case of *Yogins* properly enlightened it is but proper that *Knowledge* having produced in them supreme *Vairâgya* they do not care for the *Guṇas* which also assume a state of equilibrium and produce no effect.

XVI. Nor are objects the result of a single mind; (for) what should become of them when not cognised by that mind.*

It may be granted that things do exist apart from the mind, but it may still be argued that they do not exist independently

* This *Sutra* is not found in the text adopted by Bhoja.

of the act of cognising. This aphorism is proposed to solve this difficulty. Whence is the object produced? If from the cognising agent, it may further be asked whether it is one mind that produces the object or many. If one, the existence of an object thought of in a moment preceding the thought of another object, cannot be possible. This, however, is not the case, for even when my mind has ceased to think of an object it is possible for the mind of my friend to think of the very same object at any subsequent time; as also for me to recognise the self-same object when I should again recur to it. It is impossible for objects to be the result of many minds inasmuch as it is a rule with respect to all mental creations, as dreams, that they should be the result of a single mind. Hence objects cannot be said to be the result of the cognising agent.

XVII. In consequence of the necessity of being tinged by them, things are known or unknown to the mind.

This philosophy holds that the mind is all-pervading. When it is established that objects exist apart from the mind it must follow from the nature of mind that it must be able to cognise all things at all times. This, however, is not so. The mind cognises objects only when it is tinged with their reflection, so to speak. Properly speaking, the mind takes the form of the object it sees, and mental perception follows. It will be seen further that knowledge arises when the mind receives a double impression, that is to say, when it is influenced by *Puruśa* on the one hand, and by the object on the other, but the explanation given here is enough to show why simultaneous perception of all possible things is not possible, the all-pervading character of the mind (and the senses) notwithstanding.

XVIII. The functions of the mind are always known, on account of the constant nature of its lord, the *Puruṣa*.

The preceding considerations about the theory of mental cognition imply that the mind is subject to tranformation. It would then follow that the soul (*Puruṣa*), the cause of all knowledge, is also subject to such transformation. The real point at issue is, that the idea of a *Puruṣa* as superior to the mind is redundant, for the mind alone is sufficient for all purposes. This is denied. It is exactly because *Puruṣa*, the lord, that is to say, the ever-present witness of the mind, is not subject to such change, that the various functions of the mind are always known. The rule is that those things which assume many forms are said to be subject to change with respect to any other which is the unchanging witness of their forms. The mind itself is unconscious, and the fact of its being ever conscious, whatever the form of its consciousness, is evidence that there is a higher witness beyond itself. This is the ever-immutable *Puruṣa*. If the *Puruṣa* were mutable, the fact of uninterrupted consciousness will share the same fate as all ordinary perceptions described in the preceding aphorism. But we are sure that consciousness is neither suspended nor modified even for a second. Hence the existence of the immutable *Puruṣa*.

XIX. Nor is it self-illuminative, for it is a perceptible.

Though the existence of *Puruṣa* apart from the mind is established, still it may be possible to dispense with it altogether, if we assume the mind to be self-illuminative, instead of non-intelligent. This the aphorism asserts cannot be. The reason is that the mind is a perceptible. The rule about the perceiver and the perceptible or the seer and the seen laid down in the preceding aphorism may be called to memory. The mind as being capable of presenting itself in *many forms*, which are all cognised by the *Puruśa* without suffering any change, can never be the ultimate, that is, self-illuminative, perceiver.

XX. Moreover, it is impossible to cognise two things at one and the same time.

The point is that the preceding considerations leave no doubt as to the mind's being not made up of mere moments (*Kśaṇa)* as the *Bauddhas* hold. This assumption, besides being untenable, will not help at all in dispensing with the existence of the *Puruśa.* If it were so, it would be impossible for any one to be conscious of both, the mind and the object, cognised by it in any the same moment of time. For if the mind were but a mere succession of momentary states, *two* different cognitions cannot be the subject of any *one* momentary consciousness. Again if objects are the result of the mind, even then such experience cannot follow: for the cognising mind is not present at the moment when it becomes the object to be cognised. Nor again could a belief in the separate existence of objects solve the difficulty. For in that instance the mind will never be able to cognise objects on account of being never identified with them, by its momentary nature. If the mind were able to cognise even without relation, then it ought to be assumed as all-knowing, which is absurd. Hence it is idle to maintain that the mind can by any subtlety of reasoning be made to displace its ever-present cogniser the *Puruśa.*

XXI. If cognition by another mind (be postulated) there would be an infinity of cognisers, and confusion of memory also.

The last resource to dispense with the existence of the *Puruśa* is to hold that every individual is possessed of many minds which cognise one another. This, however, cannot be. If one mind cognises another, that ought to be cognised by a third, and the third by a fourth, and so on *ad infinitum.* This would involve the argument of *regressus ad infinitum.** Nor could the number of minds be limited and the relation of cogniser and cognised defined among them; for the necessity and number of cognising minds can never be ascertained. There would moreover be utter confusion of memory by assuming an infinity of minds. On the recollection of a set of circumstances peculiar to one mind there would arise with it a train of concomittant circumstances extending into infinity and would prevent all discriminate memory of any act. Hence it is useless to try to dispense with the existence of the *Puruśa.*

XXII. When the never-changing soul takes its form, then arises knowledge of its own cognition.

Having established that the soul exists apart from the mind, it is proposed to explain how the mind cognises itself and its environments. The soul (*Puruśa*) is never subject to any change, but it is reflected, so to speak, in the mind, and takes, as it were, through this reflection, the form of the thinking principle. Through the power of this reflection the mind is enkindled into consciousness, and performs acts of cognition. The reflection does not necessarily mean an actual reflection, but the spontaneous magnet-like influence of the soul on the mind. The soul is, for convenience of explanation, regarded as having two powers of intelligence: the ever-present (*Nityodita*) and the manifest (*Abhivyangya*). The former is ever its own but it, the latter that is capable of influencing the mind.

XXIII. The mind tinged by the seer and seen has everything for its subject.

The preceding explanations being over, it is proposed to explain the nature of mental perception; and to explain along with it how certain philosophers are led to regard objective existence as merely a function of the mind. The mind is modified in a double manner, and knowledge arises only when this double modification is simultaneous. It is influenced, on the one hand, by the soul and rendered capable of cognising; and it is affected by objects presented to it on the other, that is to say, it takes the form of the objects it sees. This double modification has, as its result, the cognition of any particular object or thought. Several philosophers consider too exclusively one or other side of the mind and deceive themselves into the belief, for example, that objects are nothing more than mere mental creations. This explanation of the process of mental cognition is intended to show how to suppress the various transformations of the mind, and how, above all, to distinguish the eternal *Puruśa* from it, and devote oneself entirely to him by entire attention to his influence.

XXIV. Though variegated by innumerable *vâsanâs*, it acts for another, for it acts in association.

If the mind does all, the *Puruśa* appears more as a redundant philosophical idea than a clear necessity. It is replied that it is not so. The mind, though full of countless impressions, is unable to act of itself, for it is only under proper external circumstances, called "association" in the aphorism, that these impressions develope themselves into actuality. Moreover, the action of the mind is always unconscious, and it therefore ever subserves its supervisor, the *Puruṣa*, whose existence is thus a direct necessity. The mind is only a storehouse of *vâsanâs* ; but it is nothing more, whence the place for and necessity of the *Puruṣa.* The mind only acts for the *Puruṣa.* What Patanjali calls mind throughout is called *Prakṛti* by Kapila; and it is remarkable what an important part mind plays in this philosophy.

XXV. The cessation of the desire of knowing the nature of the soul (takes place) in one who has mastered the difference.

Having finished all metaphysical discussions about the nature of mind and soul, and having established their difference, it is now proposed to explain the nature of final emancipation or *Kaivalya.* And first, the qualifications of one who attains to it. One who has the desire to know what is the soul and what the relation his mind and the universe bear to her, is said to be desirous of *Kaivalya.* When such a person clearly experiences the distinction between mind and soul, and understands the powers and nature of either, the said desire is extinguished within him. *Kaivalya* is, in fact, a state in which there is entire cessation of all desire, and when the nature of the essence of all consciousness is known, there is no room for any action of the mind, the source of phenomena.

This aphorism is interpreted in a different manner by *Bhoja.* He says that one who has known clearly the difference between mind and soul, loses that false knowledge whereby he used to regard his mind as soul. I have followed the *Maṇi-prabhâ* of Râmânanda-Sarswati in my explanations, for the obvious reason that the intention of the aphorism is more than a mere denial of the mind's being taken for the soul. This has indeed been effected by the preceding aphorisms, and the point here seems to be to explain the result of that conviction. To merely repeat an affirmation of this distinction by way of the intended result, appears but a poor compensation of *Yoga*-efforts, in comparison to the grand idea of the cessation of all desire, even the desire of knowing the soul.

XXVI. Then the mind is bent towards discrimination and is full of *Kaivalya*.

The state of the mind of such a *Yogin* is now described. The mind, before such knowledge, was bent towards worldly objects, but now it is entirely bent on discriminative knowledge. This knowledge is of the kind of clear cognition of the difference between mind and soul. Not only this but the mind is entirely full of the idea of *kaivalya* to the exclusion of other thoughts.

XXVII. In the breaks, there are other thoughts from impressions.

By breaks is here meant the suspension of the condition of entire devotion to the idea of *kaivalya*, described in the preceding aphorism. This is possible at the commencement. Impressions mean previous impressions, impressions of various previous incarnations.

XXVIII. Their destruction is after the manner of destroying the distrations.

Distractions and the way to get over them are already described. The rest of the meaning is clear.

XXIX. Even after illumination, there arises, in one who works without attachment, the constant flow of pure discrimination called "the cloud of merit" which is the best *samâdhi.*

The point of this aphorism is to show that even full discrimination is not the desired end, and should be superseded by supreme non-attachment which is the nearest road to *samâdhi*, the door of *kaivalya*. Illumination (*prasankhyâna*) is the light of knowledge resulting from constant discriminative recognition of the twenty-six elements of this philosophy. It is of the kind described in aphorism XLIX. Sect. III. When after this illumination the *Yogin* works entirely without attachment to any object or desire, he reaches the state of supreme non-attachment wherein the light of the soul breaks out in full. In fact all appears full of soul and there is nothing to interrupt this blissful perception. This state is of the highest merit which is compared to a cloud inasmuch as it besprinkles the germs of *samâdhi* into full bloom.

XXX. Then (follows) cessation of distractions and action.

Then, that is, when *samâdhi* is reached. The five kinds of distractions are already described. The cessation of action does not mean that all action of whatever kind is put a stop to; but it is implied that *Karma* does not affect the *Yogin*, inasmuch as it is only like seeds sown after being baked on fire.

XXXI. Then in consequence of the infinity of knowledge free from all obscuration and impurity, the knowable becomes small.

When the distractions are destroyed and when *karma* is

rendered powerless for good or ill, there arises full knowledge which is free from the obscuration caused by *rajas* and *tamas*, and cleared of all impurities arising from the said distractions. This knowledge is infinite. As compared to this infinity, that which ordinary men regard as the knowable appears but an insignificantly small thing. It is easy to know it at any time; though it is not possible that the desire to know a comparatively worthless thing should ever arise.

XXXII. Then the succession of the transformations of the *guṇas* come to an end, they having ful-filled their end.

When such knowledge arises and supreme non-attachment is at its height, there arises in the *Yogin* entire cessation of the effects of the three *guṇas*. The *guṇas* work for the *puruśa*. The *puruśa* having known himself, the *guṇas* cease to act, they having ful-filled their end. The whole universe is but a succession of transformation upon transformation of the *guṇas*. These transformations take an inverse course and are merged each into their higher source till all is reduced to matter with the three qualities *(triguṇâtmakapradhâna.)* No fresh transformations take place; and hence the succession of transformations comes to an end, in the case of the *puruśa* who has understood *kaivalya*.

XXXIII. Succession is that which is known by moments, and is cognised at the last modification.

The preceding aphorism deals with successions of transformations. It is proposed to explain what is succession. Succession implies order in time and as such its form can be known only by a knowledge of the very infinitesimal particles of time called moments (*kśaṇa.*) Again it can be known as a definite thing only when a particular tsansformation or modification takes a definite shape, that is to say, is at an end. When the succession of modifications has ceased, there is, in fact, no limit either in time or in space to the knowledge and existence of the *Yogin.*

XXXIV. The inverse resolution of the *guṇas* void of the motive to act for the *puruśa* is *kaivalya*; or it is the power of the soul centred in itself.

It is here proposed to define *kaivalya* the state to which the *Yogin* has arrived after what is described in the preceding aphorism is accomplished. It is defined in a twofold manner; from the side of *prakṛti* as also of *puruśa.* The *guṇas* always act for the soul and their object being fulfilled on the soul knowing himself, they cease to act. Their effects, the various transformations, merge each in their higher source and nothing remains for the *puruśa* to cognise. This state of the *puruśa* is *kaivalya* or the state of single-ness. It does not mean that the universe is reduced to nothing, for it continues to exist for all those who have not acquired *knowledge.* In the case of one who has acquired knowledge, the visible universe, the cause of distraction, the state of concentration, the supreme idea of non-attachment, all with their impressions, merge into the mind, which again merges into mere being, which resolves itself in *mahat,* which finally loses itself in *pradhâna.* This *kaivalya* of the *pradhâna* is, by way of metaphor said to be of the *puruśa.* Or *kaivalya* may be explained from the side of the *puruśa.* When the *puruśa* has so far received due illumination as to estrange itself from all relation with *pra-*

dhâna and its tranformations it is said to be *kaivalya*, alone, or in a state of *kaivalya*. This is the power of the soul centered in itself. *Kaivalya*, it will at once appear, is not any state of negation or annihilation, as some are misled to think. The soul in *kaivalya* has his sphere of action transferred to a higher plane limited by a limitless horizon. This our limited minds cannot hope to understand.

APPENDIX.

(Translation of Extracts from the Hathapradipikâ.)
(With brief explanations.)

"The *Hathavidyâ** should be practised entirely in private by the *Yogin* desirous of success; it conduces to power when thus practised, and becomes fruitless otherwise."—I. 2

"The practitioner of *hatha* should reside in a monastery or place which may be entirely secluded; situated in a country ruled by a good king, inhabited by religious people, affording easy means of maintenance, and free from harassment; which again should be not larger in breadth and length than the length of a bow; and should be free from stones, fire and water. The place for *yoga* is that which has a small door for egress and ingress, which is otherwise without any loopholes, and is free from crevices and holes, which is neither too high nor too low, which is clean washed with cow-dung paste, which is free from insects of all description, and which is pleasant with gardens, wells, and similar environments."—I. 12. 13.

"*Yoga* never succeeds when accompanied by excessive eating, exhaustive occupation, too much talking, adhering to painful vows, mixing in society, and fickleness of mind. It becomes successful by energy, enterprise, perseverance, knowledge of the *tattva*, resolution, and solitude."—I. 15. 16.

Yama and *Niyama* are already described in the text of Patanjali. The third stage is that of *âsana*. The *âsanas* or

---

* *Ha* means the moon and *tha* the sun, both being symbols for the two breaths. *Hathavidyâ* or *Hathayoga* is the science of regulating the breath (*prâṇa.*)

postures are said to be eighty-four in number, and each has its peculiar influence on the body and the mind. By variation of *âsanas* and kinds of *prâṇâyâma*, *yogins* get over almost all kinds of diseases. Of all the different postures four are said to be the best.

"Sit with the body perfectly straight after placing the right foot in the cavity between the left thigh and the calf, and the left foot in the cavity between the right thigh and the calf. This is called *svastikâsana.*"

"Having pressed the perinœum with the end of the left foot place the end of the right foot on the spot exactly above the penis. Then fix the chin steadily on the heart and remaining unmoved like a post, direct the eyes to the spot in the middle of the brows. This is *siddhâsana*. It is also called *vajrâsana*, *muktâsana*, or *guptâsana.*"

"In all the 84 postures always practise the *siddhâsana*, for it is that which purifies all the seventy-two thousand *nâdis.*"

"Place the left foot on the right thigh, very near the joint, and place the right foot similarly on the left thigh. Then stretching the arms backward hold the thumb of the right foot with the right hand, and that of the left with the left. Place the chin on the heart and fix the eyes on the tip of the nose sitting perfectly straight. This is the *padmâsana*, the destroyer of all diseases."

"Place the right foot in an inverted position under the right part of the perinœum and the left foot under the left part, and hold both the feet by both the hands. This is *bhadrâsana.*"—I. 19-35-37-39-44.

Having mastered one of the postures the actual practice of *yoga* may commence. "One who abstains totally from sexual intercourse, keeps temperate habits, and remains free from worldliness, becomes a *Yogin* after a full twelve-months' practice. By temperance in eating is meant the eating only three-fourths of what is actually required. The food also should consist of substantial liquids and tasteful solids. Bitter, acid, pungent, saltish, and hot things, as well as green vegetables, oil, intoxicating drugs, animal food of every description, curds, whey, etc. are to be strictly avoided. Wheat, rice barley, milk, *ghee*, sugar, butter, sugar-candy, honey, dry ginger, the five vegetables beginning with *Patol*, oats (*muga*), and natural waters, are most agreeable. In the beginning avoid fire, woman, and exertion. Young, old, decrepit, or sick, may all obtain success by steady practice. Success attends practice, none succeeds who lacks in practice: mere reading of *yoga*-books, or talking on the subject, can never conduce to success."—I. 57. 58. 59. 61—65.

"Having mastered some one posture, and observing the rules of diet etc, the *yogin* may begin the study of regulating the breath. Disturbance of mind follows disturbance of breath, and the mind remains calm when the breath is calm ; hence in order to attain fixity of mind, the breath should be controlled. So long as the *nâdis*, the vehicles of *prâṇa*, are obstructed by abnormal humours, there is no possibility of the *prâṇa* running in the middle course (*saśumṇâ*,) and of accomplishing the *unmani-mudrâ*. Hence *prâṇâyâma* should be practised, in the first instance, for the clearance of these humours. The *prâṇâyâma* for this purpose is as follows. Having assumed the *padmâsana* posture, the *yogin* should inhale at the left nostril, and having retained the breath for the time he easily can, should let it off at the opposite nostril ; and repeat the same process beginning with the nostril where he exhales. This will make one *prâṇâyâma.* These should be practised four times in twenty-four hours, in the morning, at noon, in the evening, at midnight; and should be slowly carried to eighty each time. The process in its lowest stage will produce perspiration, in its middle stage tremor, and in its highest stage levitation. The student may rub his body with the perspiration produced from the exertion; for this will make his body strong and light. In the beginning of the practice, milk and *ghee* are the best to live upon; the process being mastered, no such rule is necessary. The breath should be mastered slowly and by degrees, just as are tamed tigers bears and other wild beasts, for otherwise the rash student is sure to come to grief. Proper *prâṇâyâma* destroys all diseases, improper one produces them. When the humours of the *nâdis* are cleared the body becomes lean and beautiful, and digestion becomes keen, health ensues, the retention of the breath is done without effort, and the *nâda* within becomes audible."—II. 1—20.

Those who cannot clear their body by this process have to resort to other six processes of more or less difficulty. They are *dhauti, basti, neti, trâtaka, nauli, kapâlabhâti.* "When the *nâdis* are cleared the way of the *Susumnâ* is thrown open, and the *prâṇa* entering it, brings the mind to that steadiness which is necessary for *samâdhi.* This state is called *Unmani.* For reaching this state *Yogins* practise various kinds of *prâṇâyâma* or *kumbhakas.* They are 8 in number: *surya-bhedana, ujjâyi, sitkâri, sitali, bhastrikâ, bhrâmari, murchhâ, plâvini.* In the beginning of *puraka* the *mulabandha* should be firmly fixed, and at the end of *puraka* the *jâlandhara.* When *kumbhaka* ends both should be given up and the *uddiyâna* should accompany *rechaka.* The time for the three varies as the numbers 1, 4 and 2, which any advanced practitioner may multiply to any extent. The first kind of *prâṇâyâma* or *kumbhaka i.e* the *suryabhedana* is done as follows. Bearing all the above instructions in mind, and having taken a firm *âsana*, make *puraka* at the right nostril, and having made *kumbhaka*, make *rechaka* at the left. The student should always be careful not to prolong *kumbhaka* beyond the point where a kind of tingling sensation is felt throughout the body and especially in the head and even in the nails of the hand. Nor should he throw out the retained breath (*rechaka*) in a hurried or forcible manner; the slower it is done the better. This *suryabhedana* clears the head, cures all disorders arising from flatulence, worms &c, and opens the way of the *suśumṇâ*. The others are done in various ways and have various properties peculiar to each"—II.45—50.

As helps to *prâṇâyâma*, and even as independent practices leading to several important results and even to *samâdhi*, there are certain physico-mental postures which are called *mudrâs*. They are ten in number: *mahâmudrâ*, *mahâbandha*, *mahâvedha*, *khechari*, *uddiyâna*, *mulabandha*, *jâlandhara*, *viparitakaraṇi*, *vajroli*, *śaktichâlana*. Of these I shall describe only three. "*Uddiyâna* consists in drawing in the navel and the parts above and below it. *Mulabandha* consists in drawing in the parts of the anus, and in mentally exerting as if to draw the *apâna* upward towards the navel. The *jâlandhara* consists in pressing the chin to the heart."-III. 58-27 The object of these is clear enough. *Prâṇâyâma* has *samâdhi* as its aim, and this is not possible unless the power at the navel called *kundali* is awakened; that is to say, is made actively operative, and sent up the way of the *suśumṇâ* which is in the middle of the body between the sun-and moon-breaths. When *prâṇa* which is forced down by *puraka* unites with *apâna* which is raised up by *mulabandha*, they unite at the navel and produce by *kumbhaka* a peculiar kind of heat which sets the *kundali* into action. *Jâlandhara* helps the process of *kumbhaka* for other-wise the breath may force itself out and lead to rupture of some blood-vessel or even the heart. When *rechaka* is being done, the *uddiyâna* helps a complete clearance of the stomach and sending up of the aroused *kundali*-power.

Prâṇâyâma is followed by *pratyâhâra*, *dhâraṇâ*, *dhyâna*, *samâdhi*. These are described by Patanjali. Several works on *yoga* describe them differently to harmonise them with the practice of *hathayoga*, and explain them as degrees of *kumbhaka* varying according to the length of its duration. All this practice is pronounced as distinctly useless (vide *katha-pradi-pikâ* ch. IV. 79) unless it leads to *râjayoga* or *nirvikalpa-samâ-dhi*. *Samâdhi* is defined as the merging of the mind in the soul. When the *kuṇdali* is awakened and the *sus'umnâ* is free, there arises the possibility of what is called *chakrabheda*.* When the *yogin* becomes perfect in this practice *samâdhi* becomes easy. The highest *samâdhi* however is that which follows upon *paravairâgya* and which is never interrupted. The *yogin* realises himself everywhere and is never disturbed by any thing, not even the temptation of supreme occult powers.

There is yet another hint given in the *katha-pradipikâ* on the same subject. There is a *laya-yoga* also as there are the *Hatha- Râja-* and we may add *mantra-yogas*. This *laya-yoga* consists in fixing the attention on some internal object and becoming absorbed in it to the extent of forgetting oneself completely. The best method to begin with is absorption in

* For particulars on this subject vide my *Râja-yoga*, second edition.

the sound (*nâda*) which is heard on closing the ears. This sound when studied in this manner with application will assume various intonations and will be felt all through the body, and will lead by intent meditation to *samâdhi*.

It will thus be seen that all kinds of *Yoga* are useful in leading to the end, *Râja-Yoga*. Unless they lead to this end they are of no use whatever and are more for burden than for use. *Hatha*-and *laya*-practices, or even *mantra*-practices which consist in repeating certain formulæ in a fixed regular order with intent mental application on their meaning, are all very useful in leading to that point in *râja-yoga* whence the way is clear. The great difference between *Hatha*-and *Raja-Yoga* lies in the fact that while the one believes that *vṛtti* (mind) follows *prâṇa* (breath), the other believes that *prâṇa* follows *vṛtti*. The latter is the more correct view of the two, and experience proves the truth and utility of practices which begin with training the mind and its action.

Published by

Facsimile Publisher
Ashok Vihar, Delhi-110052 (India)
Website: www.facsimilepublishers.com

Distributed by

Gyan Books Pvt. Ltd.
5, Ansari Road, Daryaganj, New Delhi-110002 (India)
E-mail: books@gyanbooks.com, Website: www.gyanbooks.com

8 888000 209355